THINKING PHILOSOPHICALLY

THINKING PHILOSOPHICALLY

An Introduction for Students

By

FREDERICK VIVIAN

1969

CHATTO & WINDUS

LONDON

Published by
Chatto & Windus Ltd
40 William IV Street
London W.C.2

★

Clarke, Irwin & Co. Ltd
Toronto

SBN 7011 1335 9 (*net edition*)
SBN 7010 0397 9 (*non-net edition*)

© Noreen Vivian 1969

Printed in Great Britain by
Butler & Tanner Ltd
Frome and London

CONTENTS

Chapter 1 PHILOSOPHY AND LANGUAGE

Chapter 2 DEDUCTION

v

CONTENTS

Chapter 5 MORAL THEORIES

CONTENTS

Chapter 6 METAPHYSICS

Chapter 7 SOME CONCLUSIONS

PHILOSOPHY AND LANGUAGE

I. WHAT IS PHILOSOPHY?

(a) Love of Knowledge

The subjects which make up the usual school curriculum are distinguished from one another by their subject matter. History and geography, biology and chemistry, deal with different aspects of man or his environment. It is not possible to draw a rigid or precise line between them; there is a subject called 'historical geography' and another called 'bio-chemistry'; nevertheless, there is widespread agreement about the kind of work done by an historian or a geographer, a biologist or a chemist.

When we ask the question 'What is philosophy?', we find that there is no such agreement about what a philosopher does or should do. The word 'philosophy' comes from two Greek words meaning 'love of knowledge', and it was in Greece that the first great philosophers, Socrates, Plato and Aristotle, lived and taught more than two thousand years ago. For them philosophy meant not only the search for answers to those questions which are generally thought to be the special concern of the philosopher, fundamental questions about how the universe began and man's purpose within it, but also the study of natural phenomena, which is today the task of the scientist.

Until about the sixteenth century, the philosopher was both a theologian and a scientist, and if one studied anything at all it was philosophy, because all knowledge was included within its orbit. Even today some universities include scientific subjects under the general title of 'Natural Philosophy'. About four hundred years ago, however, a revolution took place in man's thinking about the world, a revolution in his conception both of what knowledge is and how it is obtained. The philosopher had believed that *real* knowledge is discovered by pure thought rather than by observation through the senses, from within rather than from without.

I

In the field of astronomy, for example, it was thought that knowledge about the heavenly bodies can be obtained without studying their movements. It seemed to the philosopher that we can be more certain that the earth is at the centre of the universe than we can be about any knowledge we receive through the senses. It could not be doubted that God had created the universe for the sake of man, and from this fact it inevitably followed that the earth must occupy a central position. When the discoveries of Copernicus, Kepler and Galileo showed that the earth was merely one of a number of planets circling the sun, they naturally provoked very strong opposition on religious grounds. Their real importance, however, lay in the way they challenged the hitherto accepted method of discovering knowledge. Basically, it was a clash between two different ideas of the way we find out what the world is like. The success which attended the theories of the new astronomy made people realize that the pure thought of the philosopher, without observation, did not lead to knowledge.

This new way of looking at the world was extended to other spheres, and produced remarkable results. The new subjects of physics, chemistry and biology were born, based on observation and experiment, but with their own special characteristics, according to their field of study.

These changes profoundly affected the position of the philosopher, who could no longer claim that philosophy provided the only avenue to knowledge. Indeed, he was destined to see his sphere of influence progressively diminished until today he readily admits that it is through science, and science alone, that true knowledge of the world can be obtained. If we want factual information, we must go to the scientist and not to the philosopher.

This inevitably prompts us to ask what can be left for the philosopher to do. What can it mean to say that philosophy is love of knowledge, if all factual knowledge is discovered by the scientist? Quite clearly, philosophy is no longer the all-embracing study it was for Plato and Aristotle, and indeed the philosopher's role has undergone fundamental changes in the last four hundred years. Nevertheless, it is true to say that his task remains the study of knowledge, although not in the way it was conceived by the philosophers of ancient Greece, nor in the way it is practised by scientists in our own day.

The scientist, by observation and experiment, discovers facts and laws, and helps us to build up our store of knowledge about the universe. The philosopher does not discover new knowledge, but analyses the knowledge we obtain from other sources. He tries to understand what we mean when we say we know something, and he makes distinctions between different kinds of knowledge. It might be said that the philosopher is one stage removed from the world of experience; his work begins only when the observations and experiments of others have been completed. The questions he asks often seem puzzling, because they are about things we normally take for granted. He does not ask whether it is true that John caught the train, but what grounds we have for thinking that people and trains really exist. He does not question whether any particular piece of knowledge about the world is true or false, but whether we can ever know anything at all about an external world. He encourages us to question many things we normally take for granted, and to puzzle over problems which we had not previously thought of as problems.

(b) Knowledge and the Senses

The most obvious source of knowledge is direct observation through the senses, knowledge of things which we can see, hear, touch, taste and smell. I know that there is a table in this room, because I can see it, that there is a clock, because I can hear it ticking, and that I am holding a pen in my hand, because I can both see it and feel it.

The philosopher is not prepared to let matters rest there; he draws our attention to certain puzzling features about the way the senses work. For example, when I say that I have a pain in the big toe of my right foot, it is because I have a sensation which I can locate in that part of my body. There surely cannot be anything which I can know more certainly than that I am feeling a pain, and that it is in my big toe.

However, a common experience of people who have had a leg amputated is that they can feel a pain in toes which they no longer have. How is it possible for someone to say that he has a pain in the big toe of his right foot, when he has no right foot? He must be mistaken, and yet his claim to know that he has the pain seems just as well founded as it was when he did in fact have a big right toe. Puzzles of this kind lead the philosopher to wonder just what happens when we see and feel things, and whether we are justified in saying that we know that they exist because we see them and feel them.

The physiologist explains the experience of 'seeing objects' by showing how light rays pass through the retina, and travel as electrical impulses along the nerves to the brain. In one sense, what we see is a picture inside our own heads, and not something outside at all. Because of this, some philosophers have maintained that objects, which we assume to exist in the outside world, are not really there, or that, if they are, we can never know that they are, because all that we can really know is what takes place within our own brains.

Bishop Berkeley, the eighteenth-century British philosopher, went so far as to maintain that things exist only when they are being observed. Thus, when I look at the table in front of me, what I am really seeing is not an object 'out there' in space, but an image inside my own head, and when I leave this room and the image of the table disappears, what I called the 'table' also disappears. In other words, there is no such thing as a table, unless there is someone to observe it. In order to modify this conclusion, which so clearly contradicts the common-sense view, Berkeley maintained that the table did have a permanent existence because it was always perceived by God.

I have chosen this example of an important philosophical problem not to decide for or against Berkeley's explanation of it, but because it brings out an essential characteristic of the things which puzzle philosophers. It is a problem which cannot be decided by finding out more about tables. The philosopher is not seeking new knowledge, but is trying to understand, more clearly and fundamentally, what we assume we already know. The kind of question he asks is not capable of being answered by the discovery of facts about the world; questions which can be answered by observation and experiment are the concern of the scientist, not the philosopher. The subject matter which he studies is not made up of things and events in themselves, but of what we claim to know about them; it is the analysis of knowledge, and not the discovery of it.

4

(c) Knowledge and Language

Whenever we express what we know, whether in speech or writing, we arrange words to form sentences. There are three types of sentence: statements, questions, and commands; but only statements convey knowledge. If I say 'Did you lock the door?', I am seeking knowledge, not giving any, and the command 'Shut the door', although it may, by implication, supply the information that I am feeling a draught, does not directly express anything I know. We can say that statements are the bricks with which the edifice of knowledge is constructed.

Therefore, in so far as philosophy is the analysis of knowledge, it is the analysis of language; but not in the way sentences are analysed in an English lesson. The student of grammar is concerned with the composition of the sentence, whereas the philosopher does not study the organization and arrangement of the sentence, but the meaning that the sentence conveys, what the sentence states. The two sentences 'It is windy' and 'Il fait du vent' are quite different, but they both state the same thing. They are two sentences, but they make only one statement. It is with statements, and not sentences, that the philosopher is concerned.

2. WORDS

(a) Symbols

There are many ways in which the language we use to talk about the world influences our picture of what the world is actually like. It is, for this reason, desirable to begin by considering some of the ways our thinking may be led astray by words, that is by a failure to understand their function.

Simultaneously with our growing up and learning what the world around us is like, we learn words so that we can refer to the things we see and touch and hear. Our primitive ancestors often failed to make any distinction between the observable properties of things and the words they used to refer to them. This was especially so with regard to proper names. They thought that to know someone's name was to know something about him in the same way as one knows the colour of his eyes or the shape of his

5

nose. A person's name was thought to be a real characteristic which could be discovered just as other personal characteristics are discovered, but one which was more fundamental and essential than those which were purely physical.

Such a belief led our ancestors to attach magical powers to names, and many primitive tribes have feared to reveal their names lest their enemies should use this most intimate knowledge to gain power over them. Every ancient Egyptian had two names, only one of which was used in everyday dealings; the other was the one by which he was known to the supernatural powers and which was revealed only to them.

It was the belief that we discover the names of people or things just as we discover their qualities that caused the lady to ask how the astronomer who first discovered the planet Uranus knew that it was so called. By careful observation we can discover the characteristics of a house or a horse, a tiger or a table, but we can never discover their names in this way. If we think about it, we shall realize that words are man-made; they are bestowed on things by man, and not discovered by him. Words are a kind of label or sign which we attach to objects for our own convenience. If I want to say something about a certain object, it is much easier to use the word 'table' than to carry the object around with me. The word 'table' is a symbol which stands for the object, table. It does not much matter what symbol is chosen; what is important is that all members of a community should use the same one. If someone chooses to have his own private system of symbols, he may derive some satisfaction from the achievement, but he will fail to communicate with anyone. It is only when there is a common system of symbols, in other words a common language, that communication is possible.

Although each separate thing does not normally have its own special symbol, we sometimes find it convenient to have one word which will refer specifically to one object or person. Such words are called 'proper names', and distinguish the individuals within a class. William Smith is a single member within the class 'man', and London is a particular town. If we attempted to do this for every individual thing in the world, one of the main purposes of language, which is to enable us to bring order into our environment, would be defeated.

6

We find ourselves in a world which is infinitely varied and complex, but by noticing that certain things have features in common, and by using symbols, or words, to refer to these features, we can sort out and arrange our impressions. Thus, words like 'man', 'animal', 'tree', 'house', enable us to reduce the multiplicity of things to manageable proportions. By using words to refer to what certain things have in common, we can arrange them in classes, ignoring those features which make every individual member of a class different from every other member. The word 'tree' can refer to every one of a large class of objects, although we know quite well that no two trees are exactly alike.

In addition to words which refer to classes of objects, we have other words, called adjectives, which refer to qualities or characteristics. A rose, a pillar-box and a sunset are very different from each other in most respects, but they may have one feature in common, namely, redness. A Dutch cheese, a discus and a mushroom are very unlike, but they all have the characteristic of being round. Still other words, called prepositions, like 'in', 'on', 'under', exist to indicate positions and relationships. Some words, such as 'of', 'unless', 'only', 'because', do not refer to anything at all and have no use by themselves, acquiring one only when they are placed in sentences with other words.

(b) Meaning

The job which a word does in the business of communication between human beings is called its meaning. But the word 'meaning' itself has very different jobs to do. We can see this if we look at the following sentences:

1. Clouds mean (are a sign of) rain.
2. When he says that, he means (is thinking of) me.
3. He says he will do it, but he doesn't mean (intend) to.
4. If you do that, it will mean (cause) trouble.
5. What does life mean (its purpose)?

We shall be concerned with a still further use of the word 'mean'. What this further use is can be seen if we notice that when we talk of the meaning of 'meaning', we place the word in quotation marks. We do this to indicate that what we are talking about is the word itself, and not about something to which the word refers. You will see this distinction more clearly if you examine the following sentences:

1. Clouds mean rain.
2. 'Clouds' mean 'visible masses of condensed watery vapour.'

The first sentence tells us something about clouds, namely, that when there are 'visible masses of condensed watery vapour' in the sky, rain is likely to follow. The second sentence, on the other hand, tells us nothing about clouds themselves, but that a certain word is used to refer to a certain atmospheric condition. Or again:

1. War produces suffering.
2. 'War' has three letters.

In the first sentence we are referring to what happens in the world, whereas in the second we are merely talking about a word.

(c) Definition

Before words can perform their primary function of enabling us to communicate with each other, it is essential that we all attach the same meanings to them. If, when I am talking to you about a table, you have a mental picture of a chair, then it is unlikely that what I am saying will make sense to you. If I say that the new table I have bought has two drawers and an oak top, it will not fit in with your picture of something to sit on. Such misunderstandings are rare between people who can be said to know a language; to know which words go with which objects is part of what is involved in knowing a language.

At the same time, we must recognize that words, by their very nature, give but an imperfect picture of the world to which they refer. Because the word 'house' can be applied to any of the millions of houses in the world, which differ from one another in an infinite number of ways, it is quite clear that the characteristics to which the word refers must be exceedingly general ones. Nevertheless, there are buildings which have some of the characteristics of houses, but which we call 'factories', and still others which we call 'shops'. To set limits to the features which a building must have before we call it a house is to define the meaning of the word 'house'.

If you want to ascertain the meaning of a word, the thing to do is to look it up in a dictionary. There the word will be defined by giving a list of its characteristics. For example, the Oxford English Dictionary says that a table is 'an article of furniture consisting of a flat top of wood, stone or other solid material, supported on legs or on a central pillar, and used to place things on or for various purposes'. If we were to give a detailed description of any of the tables we know, there would be many other features which are not included in the dictionary definition. There are tables which have baize or leather tops, tables which fold up or expand, tables with drawers, and many other kinds. But all these are extra, even if very useful, features, and the articles of furniture in question would still be tables even if these features were not present.

The definition of a word consists of a list of the characteristics which a thing must possess before the word can be correctly applied to it. These are called 'the defining characteristics'. The other features which a thing may have, but which are not essential for the word to apply, are called the 'accompanying characteristics'.

Because all things possess a very large, if not infinite, number of features, it is not always easy to decide which of them are defining and which accompanying. If an article of furniture is a flat piece of wood without legs or a central pillar, and is used to place things on, is it still a table? Or if it is a flat piece of wood with legs and is used chiefly for sitting on, is it a table or does it become a chair?

The difficulty of drawing a precise line between those characteristics which are *defining* and those which are *accompanying* illustrates an essential feature of language; this is called its 'open texture'. There are inevitably some characteristics which are not obviously one or the other. Failure to distinguish between them, however, can often lead to foolish disagreements. For example, if we were asked to give the definition of the word 'swan', one of the characteristics we might include is whiteness. Because, however, it was discovered that in Australia there are birds which resemble swans in all other respects, but are black, we have to agree that whiteness is not a defining, but an accompanying, characteristic. To refuse to change our definition of the word would be to indulge in a pointless verbal dispute.

(d) Denotation and Connotation

When we talk about the meaning of a word, we are usually thinking of its dictionary definition. Thus the meaning of the word 'bachelor' is 'unmarried male'; but we can also say that the word 'bachelor' refers to a particular class of people, namely, all those males who are unmarried. In other words, in addition to referring to those qualities or features which a person must have in order to be called a bachelor, the word 'bachelor' refers to all the people who are bachelors. The dictionary meaning of the word is called its 'connotation', whereas the whole class of persons to whom the word refers is called its 'denotation'.

There is a whole class of words which do not appear in the dictionary—proper names. This is because words like 'William', 'Mary', 'London', 'England', although they denote particular persons or places, do not have any real connotational meaning. If someone is called William, we know that he is a male, and Mary must be a female, but that is all the words connote. Proper names may have an etymological meaning, but we learn nothing about a person called Peter by being told that the word 'Peter' means 'rock'. It is because proper names have no connotational meaning that questions such as 'What is the meaning of "John Smith"?' would sound very odd.

There is also a class of words which have a connotation but do not denote anything, and this class is of some importance because it frequently gives rise to confusion of thought. A simple example of this class is the word 'unicorn', which has the connotation 'an animal which has one horn and resembles a horse', but has no denotation because unicorns have never existed. I do not imagine that many people have been led to think that, because there is a word 'unicorn', there must be an animal to which the word refers, but this is precisely the kind of mistake which has been made with many other words in our language.

Abstract words like 'truth', 'beauty', 'life' and 'will' have a dictionary meaning, that is, a connotation, and they are constantly used as if they refer to, or denote, some quality or thing which exists. We can say of someone that he is always trying to get at the truth about a question, but do we really mean that he is searching to uncover some particular characteristic or object? Is 'seeking for the truth of a question' the same sort of operation as 'looking for the key of a cupboard'? Surely it is much more like looking for beauty in a work of art. If we look at a beautiful painting, we cannot point to any part of the surface of the picture and say 'There lies the beauty'; we cannot say that it is beautiful because it possesses some particular thing or characteristic which is 'beauty'. In the same way, there is no particular thing or characteristic which is 'truth'. We can say that certain statements are true, and when we say of someone that he is seeking the truth about a question, we mean that he is seeking to discover what true statements can be made about that question. If a teacher says to a pupil who is trying to explain why he was absent, 'I want the truth', all that he wants the child to do is to make true statements which will explain why he was absent.

The beginning of Francis Bacon's famous essay 'Of Truth', ' What is truth? said jesting Pilate; and would not stay for an answer', may lead one to imagine that Pilate's question can be answered in the same way as one would answer 'What is sulphur dioxide?' or 'What is vermicelli?' To imagine so is to make the mistake of assuming that, because a word has a connotation, there must be something in the world which it denotes.

Although to give the meaning of a word is to give its connotation, there is a sense in which we can be said to know what a word means and still be unable to say precisely what that meaning is. It is true that, for those who have reached a certain state of literacy, it is the dictionary which is consulted in the search for meaning, and connotative definitions are what the dictionary provides. Nevertheless, a large number of people never consult a dictionary, and would be at a loss to give the defining characteristics of the common words they use. They know perfectly well how to use these words, without being able to analyse what they know. They are quite at home with the denotation of the words, but are puzzled when asked for their connotation.

This state of affairs is not confined to those who are not fully literate. We often feel that we know perfectly well how to use a word, but are unable to say precisely what it means. We may feel confident that we can tell poetry from mere doggerel, but when we are asked to say exactly what poetry is, we are defeated. All we can do is to say, 'This is poetry, and this is poetry, but that is not poetry.' To know the meaning of the word 'poetry' is to know where to bestow the name, and if we were to succeed in enumerating the defining characteristics of poetry, this definition could never stand up against something which we recognize as poetry but which does not fit our definition.

In the world of literature, music and painting, it is often the case that the denotation of a word takes precedence over the connotation; we find it easier to apply the labels 'classical' and 'romantic' than we do to define them.

(e) Emotive Power

The Oxford Dictionary gives the meaning of 'politician' as 'one practically engaged in conducting the business of the state', and of 'statesman' as 'one who takes a leading part in the affairs of state, esp. one who is skilled in the management of public affairs'. The difference in the connotation of 'politician' and 'statesman' is that the latter is *skilled*, and takes a *leading* part in public affairs. A politician, by becoming skilled and assuming a leading role in affairs, can achieve the status of a statesman. The fundamental difference between these two words, as they are commonly used, is not, however, fully expressed by their connotational meaning. If we call someone a statesman rather than a politician, it is because we consider that his political activities are worthy of approval. In addition to its purely connotative meaning, sometimes called its 'cognitive' meaning, the word 'statesman' has a tendency to arouse favourable emotions. We talk of someone who has served his country well as being an 'elder statesman', and of a political action of which we approve as being 'statesmanlike'. On the other hand, the word 'politician' is often used in a pejorative sense, suggesting someone who is more concerned with gaining party or even personal advantage than he is with wider national interests.

The power that some words have to arouse feelings in this way is called their 'emotive force'. It is something which some words acquire in addition to their strict connotation, or cognitive meaning. In pairs of words such as 'thrifty' and 'miserly', 'firm' and 'stubborn', the difference in meaning is far greater than can be accounted for by their cognitive meaning alone. If we approve of someone for sticking to his principles, we call him 'firm', but if we disapprove, we call him 'stubborn', or even 'pig-headed'. We can thus use the emotional force which words have to express our own feelings of approval or disapproval without explicitly stating them.

Some abstract words have a rich emotional meaning, for example 'culture', 'democracy', 'freedom', 'courage', 'chastity', and we should find it very difficult to give them a precise cognitive meaning. We should not feel very confident that we could set out all their defining characteristics, but we have no doubt that they are all used with a strong feeling of approval. We may not be quite sure what 'culture' is, but we know perfectly well that it is a good thing. Because of this, we sometimes find that in a discussion the strong emotional force attached to a word hides the fact that there is a total lack of agreement about its cognitive meaning.

The attempt is often made, especially in America, to attach the label 'socialist' or 'communist' to reforms which are disapproved of, not because they are socialist or communist by any generally accepted definition of these terms, but because it is hoped that the distaste which is felt by some people for these doctrines may become attached to the reforms.

(f) Persuasive Definitions

Abstract nouns cannot be defined with any accuracy, and the meaning which is given to them often varies from person to person, and from age to age. There is a central core of meaning which remains common and constant, but around the fringe, so to speak, there are always areas where disagreement is possible, indeed probable. In these cases we are tempted to define words in such a way as to persuade people to our own way of thinking.

These words have a tendency to retain their emotional force even though their cognitive meaning may change, and this provides a powerful instrument in moulding attitudes and interests. 'Chastity', which has a favourable emotional meaning, has usually stood for 'sexual continence outside the marriage bonds'. There is, however, a growing feeling today that this is not necessarily a virtue, and that to be unchaste, within this meaning of the word, is not necessarily a vice. In order to persuade others to this point of view, the word is retained, with all its emotional force, but the cognitive meaning is changed. Chastity, it is argued, is a very good thing, but what 'chastity' really means is not just sexual continence, but respect and love.

One is more likely to change a person's attitude to sex by a subtle re-definition of what it means to be chaste than by trying to make him adopt an unfavourable emotional response to the word 'chastity'. It will be much more difficult to make him feel that chastity is a bad thing than to get him to transfer his favourable feeling to a new definition of the word. The emotion is retained, but the meaning is changed.

The following is an extract from the *Guardian* of June 1964: 'As for Aims of Industry he said, it was not a political organization but was entirely to do with free enterprise.' The speaker wished to persuade his listeners that whether we are to have free enterprise or a controlled economy is not a political question. If 'Aims of Industry' is thought to be playing politics, it will arouse a feeling of disapproval, and this can best be avoided by giving a new definition to the word 'political'. The speaker would like to persuade his audience that economic organization should not be included in the definition of 'politics'. Such subtle forms of persuasion are often more effective than the explicit statement of a point of view, and we must always be on our guard to detect them.

Such a process, whereby we redirect a person's attitude or interest by subtly changing the meaning of a word without significantly altering its emotional force, is called 'persuasive definition'. The British and the Russians both use the favourable emotional attitude to the word 'democracy' in order to enlist support for two very different political systems. For us 'democracy' means 'one man one vote', free elections, the party system and the possibility of throwing out governments we do not like. The Russian system has some features which we should be prepared to call democratic, but it lacks what we should consider the most important of all–the power to change the system of government itself.

Because the words 'religion', 'democracy', 'freedom' are given widely different connotational meanings, one may be tempted to ask what these words *really* mean. When one person says that religion is 'morality tinged with emotion', and another excludes morality from religion altogether, should we not ask which is the *true* definition? Ever since Socrates and Plato, many philosophers have believed that one should be able to answer such a question.

When Plato asked 'What is justice?' or 'What is courage?' he was not asking for definitions of the words 'justice' and 'courage', but for an account of what justice and courage really are.

If A says that justice means absolute equality of treatment and reward, and B says that it means that everyone should get only what he deserves, they may be tempted to wonder what justice *really* is. But there is no way of answering such a question, because there is no thing called 'justice' which can be examined to provide an answer. A believes in equality of reward, and B in reward according to desert and because the word 'justice' has a favourable emotional force, they both annex it in order to strengthen their own attitudes. If, indeed, it were possible to show that A, for example, was using the word with its *true* meaning, B would not say that he must now believe in equality of reward but that he no longer believes in justice. It is because words like 'justice' have no *real* meaning that they can retain their emotional force even with different cognitive meanings.

Plato believed that it is possible to discover *real* meanings because, for him, a definition is not a definition of a word, but of a thing. However, when he claimed to have discovered the *real*, or essential, meaning of justice, he was doing nothing more than putting forward his own ideas about what he considered desirable in the organization of society. He was trying to make a persuasive definition pass for a statement of fact.

It seems clear that all such questions as 'What is the *real* meaning of . . .?' are based on the mistaken belief that definitions are of things. People who talk of the *real* meaning of 'religion', or 'democracy', or 'freedom', or other abstract words of this kind, are trying to conceal the fact that they are giving these words their own private meanings.

There is no special knowledge, or insight, which will enable us to discover the *real* characteristics of democracy, for the simple reason that there is no thing to which the word refers. We may trace the history of the word back to Greece and discover that, there, it meant a system of government in which not all adult citizens were entitled to vote, but that those who were entitled to voted in person. If 'democracy' *really* means the system of government which was practised in ancient Greece, then neither Britain nor Russia is a democracy. There is, of course, no *real*, or essential, meaning of the word, and if the British and the Russians choose to use the same word to refer to two different political systems, it means that in all conversations between them the word has ceased to have any meaning. Communication is possible only as long as they agree to define words in the same way, but it makes no sense to say that one definition is true and the other false. We cannot answer any question of fact about a democracy by analysing the word 'democracy'.

Aldous Huxley, in *Eyeless in Gaza*, shows how we are inclined to place 'true' or 'real' before any word we are proposing to re-define:

'But if you want to be free, you've got to be a prisoner. It's the condition of freedom–true freedom.'

'True freedom!' Anthony repeated in the parody of a clerical voice. 'I always love that kind of argument. The contrary of a thing isn't the contrary; oh, dear me, no! It's the thing itself, but as it *truly* is. Ask any die-hard what conservatism is; he'll tell you it's true socialism. And the brewers' trade papers; they're full of articles about the beauty of true temperance. Ordinary temperance is just gross refusal to drink; but true temperance, *true* temperance is something much more refined. True temperance is a bottle of claret with each meal and three double whiskies after dinner. . . .

'What's in a name?' Anthony went on. 'The answer is, practically everything, if the name's a good one. Freedom's a marvellous name. That's why you're so anxious to make use of it. You think that, if you call imprisonment true freedom, people will be attracted to the prison. And the worst of it is you're right.'

3. ANALYSIS OF CONCEPTS

When we ask the questions 'What is culture?', or 'What is art?', or 'What is democracy?', we are seeking a definition of a word. We want to know to what characteristics it is proposed that these words shall refer, because they are often vague and constantly changing. There is another type of question, however, which presents us with a different kind of problem. Questions like 'What is responsibility?', or 'What is free will?', or 'What is causality?' are not to be answered merely by defining the terms used. We do not have to decide just how we propose to use these words, but rather what meaning we can conceivably give them. We are not presented with the problem of prescribing limits to their meaning, but of deciding whether they have any meaning and, if so, what it can be.

We constantly use words like 'responsibility', 'free will', and 'causality', but do we really know what we mean when we use them? The problem they present is not one of choosing between various clear, alternative definitions, but rather of dispelling a fog of imprecision and muddle with which they seem to be surrounded. The elucidation of the puzzles which words of this kind present is one of the main tasks still left to the philosopher.

If we say 'John chose to study medicine of his own free will', we mean that no pressure was brought to bear on him by his parents, school masters or anyone else to pursue that particular career. The idea of becoming a doctor appealed to John; he felt that this was what he wanted to do, and no one pushed him into it against his wishes. This is the kind of thing we mean when we say that we do something of our own free will. If John had said, 'I did not want to become a doctor; my ambition was to be a concert pianist, but father insisted that I follow him into the medical profession', we should say that John had not acted of his own free will.

The distinction between these two cases is perfectly clear, and there is no difficulty in understanding what is meant by saying that we sometimes do things of our own free will, and sometimes do not. We say that our wills are free whenever we are able to do those things we want to do, and are not free when we are impeded or impelled by forces outside ourselves. But if we analyse the concept of 'free will' a little further, we shall find that this distinction is not at all clear-cut.

When John chose to become a doctor, he did so presumably because his knowledge of what a doctor's life is like prompted in him certain favourable desires, but we also believe that these desires can be explained as the result of the interaction of John's temperament and environment. That is, we believe that these desires did not arise spontaneously and uncaused, but are what they are because John is the kind of person he is. If we want to understand why John is that kind of person, we must look for the answer by tracing back his life history. If we do this, we shall discover a long causal chain, stretching back to his birth, and even beyond. John inherited his physical and mental endowment from his parents, and this was developed and moulded by the environment into which he was born. Must we not, therefore, say that, although John chose to be a doctor of his own free will, at the moment of choice there was nothing else he could have done, being the kind of person he was? Unless we are prepared to abandon the idea that all events have causes, even in the mental sphere, can we avoid the conclusion that, in another sense of 'free will', John could not have chosen any other course?

By digging beneath the surface of the concept of 'free will', we have unearthed one of the biggest and most important of philosophical puzzles. However we attempt to explain the philosophical problem, we can still make the significant distinction between actions which are done as the result of a person's own desires and those which are brought about by pressures from outside. We can still say that some actions are the result of free will, and some are not.

We find a similar problem when we analyse the concept of responsibility. We all use the words 'responsible' and 'responsibility', and are probably unaware that they present any particular difficulty. To say that William was responsible for breaking the window is to say that it was William who threw the stone which caused the glass to break. But we may know that a person committed the murder of which he is accused, and still ask whether he was responsible for his action. We are not asking if he was the cause of the crime, since we know that he was; we are asking whether he was suffering from some mental illness which deprived him of the power of choice.

Psychologists tell us that there are mental diseases which are so compulsive that their victims have no power to resist. A kleptomaniac is just such a person. Because of a serious mental derangement, he, or more usually she, is driven to steal articles he does not want. If we believe that 'responsible for' never means anything more than 'is the cause of', we shall never understand someone who says 'The kleptomaniac is not really responsible for his actions.'

It is with the elucidation of puzzles such as these that the philosopher is primarily concerned. John Locke, a British philosopher of the seventeenth century, fully understood this problem when he wrote: 'The greatest part of the questions and controversies that perplex mankind depend on the doubtful and uncertain use of words.'

4. STATEMENTS

(a) Meaning of 'True' and 'False'

The words 'true' and 'false' are both used in different ways with different meanings. Here are some examples:

1. He showed true (sincere) emotion.
2. He was a true (loyal) friend.
3. The ground wasn't true (smooth, level).
4. The breed has remained true (unchanged).
5. He is the true (rightful) heir.

If we examine the use of 'true' in the above examples, we notice that in every case it describes a quality of something–the sincerity of an emotion, the loyalty of a friend, the smoothness of the ground. There is another sense of 'true' which does not describe a thing, but a statement. For example, in 'It is true that President Kennedy was assassinated' and 'It is true that a triangle has three sides', it is not the President or the triangle which is true but what is said about them, namely the statements 'President Kennedy was assassinated' and 'A triangle has three sides.'

Things and people exist and events take place, but they cannot be said to be true or false. A table can be round or square, made of wood or of metal, but it cannot be true or false. If I say that a table is round when it is square, then my statement is false, but the table cannot be false. A concert can be exciting or dull, of short or of long duration, and anything I say about it may be true or false, but not the concert itself. In the sense in which we shall use the words, the only things which can be said to be true or false are statements.

(b) Verification and Falsification

If someone had asked us soon after the event how we knew that President Kennedy had been assassinated, we should probably have replied that we had heard it announced on the radio or had read it in the paper. We should have given an account of the way we became acquainted with the information. But if our questioner had persisted and had asked how we knew that the statement was true, we should have replied that, in a matter of such gravity, the B.B.C. or the newspaper can be relied upon to tell the truth. We were prepared to accept the truth of the statement on the authority of the B.B.C. or of the newspaper.

The bulk of our knowledge is made up of statements whose truth we accept because they issue from some authoritative source. When we are very young our parents are the sources of knowledge, and as we get older teachers and books of reference, to a large extent, replace parents. On the whole, we believe that the information we receive in this way is reliable; our parents and teachers and even books of reference may sometimes be wrong, but we assume they do not deliberately mislead. If a geography master tells us that there are vineyards along the 'Côte d'Or', we probably accept it as true, solely on the grounds that he is an expert in his subject. Anyone who still feels sceptical about it can consult a book on the geography of France, thereby exchanging one authority for another.

We rely for the truth of the greater part of the information we acquire on the authority of persons or books. I do not wish to suggest that there is anything undesirable in such an arrangement, but to accept a piece of information as being true because someone says so does not mean that it is also the reason why it is true. It is of the utmost importance that we should distinguish between the actual way we learn that statements are true and the reasons or grounds for believing them to be true. In practice, we often accept the truth of statements on someone's authority, but they are not true just because someone says they are. There is no statement whose truth can ultimately be based on the authority of any person.

It is one of the philosopher's main tasks to examine the various ways we can decide whether statements are true or false, that is, how we can verify or falsify them. If I ask someone to verify that a train leaves at 10.15 a.m., he will understand that this involves consulting the railway time-table. To verify that $175 \times 139 = 24,325$, it is necessary to work carefully through the multiplication sum. If I get the same result on several occasions, I shall feel justified in assuming that it is correct and that the statement is true.

Not all statements are so straightforward. Most people would consider 'It is right to keep promises' to be true, but it is not at all clear what kind of test we should apply to verify it. It is the job of the philosopher to formulate the different tests to which we must subject statements before we are justified in accepting them as true. These tests are not all the same and, as we shall see, there are some statements which seem to have a meaning but which elude all attempts at verification or falsification. Nevertheless, it is by looking at statements in this way, by asking how we can tell whether they are true or false, that we can often elucidate just what a particular statement means or, more precisely, what someone means when he makes it.

(c) Different Types of Statement

Let us now consider four different types of statement and the ways in which they can be verified.

(i) All bachelors are unmarried.
(ii) There are lions in Africa.
(iii) It is wrong to break promises.
(iv) The soul is immortal.

(i) 'All bachelors are unmarried'

One's first reaction to such a statement is that it does not need to be verified because it is so obviously true. 'Bachelor' is a name we apply to all men who are not married, and to say that all bachelors are unmarried is the same as saying that all unmarried men are unmarried. If we deny that this is true, we contradict ourselves. The second part of the sentence analyses the meaning of the first part, and for this reason statements of this kind are called 'analytic'. We can see automatically that they are true, provided we understand the meaning of the words.

(ii) 'There are lions in Africa'

We cannot decide whether this is true or false by analysing what the words mean. There is nothing in the meaning of the word 'lion' which makes it inevitable that there should be lions in Africa.

To verify this statement it would be necessary to go to Africa and travel around until we actually saw a lion. We should verify it by means of our senses, the most important of which would be that of sight. We might hear or smell something which would make us think that lions were present, but if we saw them as well, we should feel more certain that we had verified their presence. Statements of this kind, which are verified by sense experience, are called 'empirical'. To contrast them with those which are called 'analytic', they are sometimes called 'synthetic'.

(iii) *'It is wrong to break promises'*

Although we should be very surprised, and perhaps a little shocked, if anyone denied this statement, it is not at all clear how we should set about verifying it. We frequently make statements of this kind, in which we seem to be more concerned to indicate that we attach value to something or to express an attitude than to make a simple statement of fact. For example, 'Shakespeare was a great dramatist' and 'Schweitzer was a good man' are not analytic, for we could deny them both without contradicting ourselves, nor are they empirical, because they cannot be verified by sense experience. We know how to verify 'Shakespeare wrote *Hamlet*' but not 'Shakespeare was a great dramatist'; we know how to demonstrate the truth of 'Schweitzer died in 1965' but not the truth of 'Schweitzer was a good man'. It would not be difficult to get two people to agree about the date of Schweitzer's death, but it would be quite a different matter if they disagreed about his goodness.

Some philosophers maintain that we possess a special faculty, or insight, which enables us to tell whether statements of this kind are true or false. They say that, in addition to the senses by which we verify ordinary empirical statements, human beings possess an additional faculty which reveals to them non-empirical qualities, such as artistic or moral worth. It is suggested that as we study the works of Shakespeare we become aware, by a process of intuition, of a certain quality which we call 'greatness'; as we read of the life of Schweitzer we discover a quality in his actions which we call 'goodness'.

There are other philosophers who do not accept this explanation, but say that these are not really statements at all. They take the view that 'Schweitzer was a good man' is not a statement of fact, but merely an expression of an attitude to the life of Schweitzer. When we read of the things he did, we find ourselves approving of the way he devoted himself to the relief of suffering. 'Schweitzer was a good man' is more like saying 'Well done, Schweitzer!' If this is so, then it is not really a statement at all but an evaluative judgement, because we are evaluating Schweitzer rather than stating anything about him which can be true or false.

We must postpone until a later chapter further discussion of these two different points of view, and with it the important problem of the verification of what some call 'value statements' and others 'value judgements'.

(iv) 'The soul is immortal'

This is not obviously true, as are analytic statements. To deny that the soul is immortal is not to contradict oneself, for there is nothing in the meaning of the word 'soul' from which it automatically follows that it is immortal. Nor does it seem to be the kind of statement which can be verified by sense experience. Spiritualists claim that they have some evidence for a belief in life after death, but these claims are not generally considered to be justified. If we are not prepared to accept the empirical evidence of the spiritualist, what other method is open to us of verifying statements of this kind? How indeed can we find the answers to a whole range of questions which man has asked from the time he first became aware of the mystery of human destiny? Man's sense of awe and wonder prompts him to ask questions about God and immortality and the purpose of life, but there is no agreement as to how they should be answered.

Problems of this kind are called 'metaphysical', and the study of them is called 'metaphysics'. The word 'metaphysics' stands for a Greek phrase meaning 'the books next after the "Physics" ', and was used by the editors of the works of Aristotle to stand for certain books which came after the main body of his scientific work. That is, the word refers to the position and not to the content of these books. Nevertheless, there is a sense in which the subject matter of metaphysics also lies 'beyond physics' and beyond other scientific studies.

Metaphysical statements are essentially statements which give the appearance of being empirical, but which cannot be shown to be true or false by the methods usually applied to such statements. They may be divided into two classes:

(*a*) Those which are concerned primarily with such questions as immortality and the existence of God, and claim to describe a supernatural or transcendental reality.

(*b*) Those which are presuppositions about the world of ordinary experience; as, for example, the belief that there is a fundamental order in nature. This is something which cannot be proved, but which is an assumption or presupposition of all scientific enquiry.

In the following chapters we shall look more closely at these four different kinds of statement in an attempt to discover the different ways they contribute to the sum of human knowledge.

(*d*) *Analytic and Empirical*

We have already seen that the only information contained in analytic statements is about the words used; they can be seen to be true by the analysis of the language in which they are expressed. Observation and experiment are in no way relevant to their truth. The truths of logic and mathematics are of this kind. We all know that '2 plus 2 equals 4' is true, without conducting any experiments; in fact, if we were to do so we might be surprised at the results. For example, if we take two drops of water and add to them two more drops, we get one drop of water and not four. Again, if we add 2 pints of alcohol to 2 pints of water we do not get 4 pints of the mixture; owing to the peculiar properties of these two liquids, we get less than 4 pints when they are mixed.

Mathematical truths are quite independent of what happens in the world we inhabit. They would be just as true in a universe where the natural laws were quite different from our own, for the simple reason that we have ourselves decided what they are. '2 plus 2 equals 4' is not a truth about the world which we have discovered, but one which we have ourselves manufactured.

(*e*) *Necessary and Contingent*

When analytic statements are true, we say that they are necessarily true, because to deny their truth would involve us in a contradiction. 'All bachelors are unmarried' is necessarily true, because a bachelor is, by definition, unmarried. To deny the truth of this would lead us to say 'All unmarried males are not unmarried males', which is a contradiction.

Unlike analytic statements, empirical statements do give us information about the world, and we say that their truth is contingent: that is, dependent upon what the world happens to be like. A false empirical statement could not be true without the world being different from what it in fact is. If I say that there is a cat in the larder, you can verify it by going and having a look. If you examine the larder carefully and do not find a cat, you will come to the conclusion that the statement is false. It cannot be true without the situation in the larder being different from the one you find. You may accept the statement as true without taking the trouble to go and find out for yourself but, whether you go or not, you know the kind of evidence which is required in order to verify or falsify it.

We may deny the truth of an empirical statement without involving ourselves in a contradiction. There is no logical reason why 'There are lions in Africa' should be true or false, and if we were to say 'There are no lions in Africa' it would be empirically false, but we should not be contradicting ourselves. We are often prepared to accept the truth of empirical statements without personally verifying them; but we do know that they are the kind which can be verified.

Most of the statements we make day by day are empirical, and school subjects like the sciences, history and geography consist largely of statements of empirical fact. They are descriptive of different aspects of the world, past, present or future, and it is by observation or experiment that we come to accept them as true or false. But they are never necessarily true, as are those of logic and mathematics.

Thus we have an important distinction between the *necessary* truth of analytic statements, which could not conceivably be otherwise, and the *contingent* truth of empirical statements, which describe the world as it is, but which could conceivably be quite different.

(f) Analytic or Empirical?

Failure to distinguish between analytic and empirical statements often leads to misunderstanding and faulty argument. When someone says 'All gardeners use spades when they dig', the statement has the appearance of being empirical; it gives us information about a class of people we call gardeners. My own experience of gardeners, however, leads me to the conclusion that it is not true, because I know several gardeners who do their digging with a fork. When I produce this new evidence, I am met with the reply 'If the people you are talking of dig with forks, they can't be gardeners'. What has happened in this little exchange? I assumed that the original statement was empirical, thus giving factual information which could be verified or falsified by observation, whereas it was analytic, giving nothing more than the speaker's definition of the word 'gardener'. If I define a gardener as someone who digs with a spade, then 'All gardeners dig with spades' is equivalent to 'All people who dig with spades dig with spades', which is logically true and cannot be falsified by evidence. But it does not tell us anything about the real world of gardeners of whom, according to the usual definition of the word, some dig with forks and others with spades.

Another example of this kind of error, and one which has far-reaching and sometimes very unfortunate consequences, is the statement 'What will be will be'. This is quite clearly analytic, because we cannot deny its truth without contradicting ourselves. All that it says is that the future tense of the verb 'to be' is the same as the future tense of the verb 'to be', and this is not something which we can deny. Why is it, then, that anyone should bother to say something which is so obviously empty of meaning? The reason is that anyone who says it does not imagine for one moment that it is meaningless. What he thinks he is saying is that our future as individuals, or the future of the world, is already decided and there is nothing we can do to change it. What he is doing is taking a statement which is analytic, and which consequently tells us nothing about the world, and then trying to persuade us to accept it as empirical, stating a matter of fact. What he thinks he is saying is 'Human actions do not influence the course of events.' This is indeed empirical, but one which most people would reject as being false.

The power we have to mould our own destiny is limited, but no one would deny that there are many ways in which each of us does control events. Every decision we take and every action we perform does, in some way, produce changes in our environment which would not have occurred if we had not taken that decision, or performed that action. This we all know to be true from our own experience, and we should not be prepared to accept any statement which clearly said otherwise. Unless we are careful, however, we may be prepared to accept it when it is not clearly stated but put forward as something which follows logically from another statement which is obviously true. 'What will be will be' is a logically true, analytic statement; 'Human actions do not influence the course of events' is empirical and is false, and there is no logical connection between them.

The belief that such a connection does exist gives rise to fatalism, a doctrine which makes a strong appeal to certain temperaments. It is often said that we believe what we want to believe, and no doubt the attraction of fatalism for some people will outweigh any proof that their belief rests upon a logical fallacy.

We must always be on our guard against believing that the obvious truth of an analytic statement can be used as evidence for an empirical one. When we are in doubt whether a statement is analytic or empirical, we must ask ourselves how we should set about verifying it. If the truth depends on the result of observation or experiment, then it is empirical; if it depends on the correct use of language, then it is analytic.

5. REASONING

We have been considering how we know that particular analytic or empirical statements can be true, but we frequently claim to know the truth of statements which go beyond the direct evidence of our senses. From perceiving something to be the case, we can go on to infer that something else is the case, that is, something additional to what we actually perceive. Thus we may hear a certain kind of sound and infer that a motor car has just gone down the road. We claim to know something beyond what we actually heard. We may smell a certain odour, and infer that someone is smoking a pipe. If we go into a shop with a pound and spend five shillings, we may infer that when we have replaced the change we have fifteen shillings left in our pockets. From the knowledge that one statement is true, we can by a process of reasoning infer that some other statement is true.

The various ways in which we are justified in making inferences form an important branch of logic. The logician is not interested in how we arrive at these inferences, for these are thought processes which are the concern of the psychologist; what concerns the logician is whether or not we are justified in making them. It is the relationship between statements, and the reasoning which leads from one to another, which the logician studies.

When we look at the following statements:

(a) 1. This plane figure is a triangle.
     2. The sum of its angles is 180°.

we see immediately, if we know anything about triangles, that these two statements are related. In fact, we know that if the first is true, then the second is also true; that is, there is a logical relationship between them.

Now look at the following:

(b) 1. This bar is made of iron.
     2. This bar will sink if placed in water.

We have all had experience of what happens when a bar of iron is placed in water. From what we have observed in the past, we feel pretty certain that it will sink to the bottom.

In both pairs of statements, a and b, we are aware that there is a relationship which enables us to say that, if the first statement is true, the second is also true. Nevertheless, the relationship between each pair of statements is not the same. It is quite impossible that a figure should be a triangle without the sum of its angles being 180°: having angles which total 180° is almost a defining characteristic of a triangle. On the other hand, although all the iron bars we have ever come across have always sunk when placed in water, it is not logically impossible that we might some day find a bar of iron which floated.

These pairs of examples illustrate the two main ways in which we can arrange statements in order to form an argument. We derive (a)2 from (a)1 by a process which we call *deduction*, and we derive (b)2 from (b)1 by a process which we call *induction*.

In a reasoned argument, we do not usually place statements one after another as we did above but indicate the way one follows from the other by the use of conjunctions such as 'If . . . then . . .' or 'Because . . . therefore . . .' When a statement is of the form 'If . . . then . . .', it is called 'hypothetical', and the clause introduced by 'if' is the 'antecedent' and the 'then' clause is the 'consequent'. We shall be able to obtain a better understanding of the difference between deductive and inductive reasoning if we study some examples.

1. If Smith is a novelist, then he is a writer.
2. If you don't wear your hat, you will catch a cold.
3. If Jones wastes his time, he will fail his examination.
4. If Brown is your father's brother, then he is your uncle.
5. If the three sides of a triangle are equal, the three angles are also equal.
6. If he goes to the party tonight, he will get drunk.

Even if we accepted all the above statements as true, it is quite clear that we should feel much more certain about some than others. If Smith is a novelist, he must write novels and must, therefore, be a writer. He could be a writer without being a novelist, but it is impossible for him to be a novelist and not, at the same time, be a writer. We may say that, if the antecedent is true, the consequent is necessarily true.

On the other hand, although people may sometimes catch cold as the result of not wearing a hat, it is not true that this always happens. We should probably all make different estimates of the chances of not wearing a hat causing a cold, but we should probably agree that there is nothing certain about it. There is no necessary connection between the antecedent and the consequent.

The first example is a piece of deductive reasoning. Once we understand the meaning of 'novelist' and 'writer', we see immediately the truth of the conclusion because the conclusion is really an analysis of the meaning of the word 'novelist'. The second example is a piece of inductive reasoning, where the relationship between the antecedent and the consequent is a causal one. We may feel inclined to accept the truth of the consequent, but it is not necessarily true.

Of the remaining examples, we notice that two are deductive and two inductive. The meanings of the words 'father', 'brother' and 'uncle' guarantee that Brown is your uncle if he is the brother of your father. Also, we can show by a simple geometrical theorem that all equilateral triangles must have equal angles. The fourth and fifth examples are, therefore, deductive.

The other two examples are inductive. We may feel convinced that unless Jones works much harder he will fail, but we should admit that there is never anything certain about examinations. Here the relationship between the antecedent and the consequent is a causal one, and it gives us no justification for feeling very sure about the outcome. In the last example the relationship is again causal, and the conclusion is no more certainly true than the other.

Deduction, which is the kind of argument or reasoning we find in logic and mathematics, gives conclusions which, if true, are necessarily true. They are true in the same way as analytic statements are true—there is nothing in the consequent which is not already present in the antecedent. Inductive reasoning, on the other hand, resembles empirical statements—it is concerned with the world of experience and provides us with new knowledge.

FOR DISCUSSION AND ESSAYS

1. 'A philosopher is a scientist who is too lazy to work in a laboratory.' Discuss.
2. 'Philosophy consists in seeking to elucidate puzzles which haunt men's minds in a way quite different from perplexities within the field of some special science.' (Sir Isaiah Berlin)
3. 'Philosophy is the activity of making clear to people what they can, and what they cannot, say.'
4. 'That all sound philosophy should begin with an analysis of propositions (statements) is a truth too obvious, perhaps, to demand a proof.' (Bertrand Russell)
5. Language is the dress of thought.
6. Criticize the following:
   a. You can never step into the same river twice because the water is always changing.

  b. It is not a bird because it cannot fly.

  c. It cannot be a town because it has fewer than 1000 inhabitants.

  d. He is not educated if he knows no science.

7. What do you think of the answer of the student who, on being asked to prove that 'the sun will rise tomorrow', answered, 'The sun will rise tomorrow because it is already tomorrow at some places on the earth, and at these places the sun has already risen.'?

8. Distinguish between the following:

  a. What exactly is lightning?

  b. What do you mean by saying he is responsible?

  c. What is cybernetics?

  d. What is beauty?

9. 'True culture is not acquaintance with the arts, but with science and technology.' Discuss.

10. It is irrelevant to attempt to discover what democracy 'essentially' means.

11. To which of the four classes—analytic, empirical, value judgement, metaphysical—do the following belong?

  a. Wood floats on water.

  b. God loves all his creatures.

  c. Cows are herbivorous.

  d. It is right to tell the truth.

  e. All triangles have three sides.

  f. Mammals suckle their young.

  g. You ought to help the poor.

  h. Liberals support proportional representation.

  i. Every event has a cause.

  j. Good drivers never drink and drive.

  k. The atomic weight of gold is 197·2.

  l. Bishops wear gaiters.

  m. Honesty is the best policy.

  n. All religions hold to a belief in God.

12. Which of the following pieces of reasoning are deductive and which inductive?

  a. You will miss the train unless you hurry.

  b. If it rains any more the match will be cancelled.

  c. If the chess piece is a bishop it will move diagonally.

d. If you practise your scales regularly your playing will improve.
e. You must be Joan's brother because she is your sister.
f. No figure is a square unless it has four equal sides.
g. If prices continue to rise there will be demands for higher wages.
h. If it is a robin it will have a red breast.

CHAPTER 2

DEDUCTION

Whenever we attempt to justify statements by producing evidence or giving reasons for them, we must make use of either deduction or induction, or a combination of both. It is, therefore, important to understand some of the principles underlying these two types of argument, so that we may be able to judge whether or not our own conclusions or those of others are justified.

We have already pointed out that both deduction and induction involve arranging certain kinds of statement in such a way that we can infer a conclusion from them. In order to illustrate how this is done in a deductive argument, it will be convenient to divide statements into two classes—categorical and hypothetical.

I. CATEGORICAL AND HYPOTHETICAL STATEMENTS

If we state something categorically, we mean that there are no 'ifs' or 'buts' about it; we are making an unqualified assertion. We sometimes deny categorically when we wish to be particularly emphatic about something, but, in the sense in which we shall use the word, there is no suggestion of unusual emphasis. 'John has passed his examination', 'Some men are lazy', 'All negroes have curly hair' are all categorical statements. The real meaning of 'categorical' can best be understood when it is compared with that class of statements called 'hypothetical' or 'conditional'.

Hypothetical statements are made up of two parts, one of which states that something is true on condition that what is stated in the other part is also true. For example, 'If you go out in the rain, you will get wet.' I am not stating categorically that you will get wet, but that you will get wet if you go out in the rain. I am stating what will happen if a certain condition is fulfilled, what will happen in an imagined, or hypothetical, situation.

2. CATEGORICAL ARGUMENTS

These two types of statement, categorical and hypothetical, may be used to form deductive arguments. If, for example, I believe that all bald men make bad husbands and that Mr. Smith is bald, then I am justified in inferring that Mr. Smith will make a bad husband. If a certain quality is possessed by all the members of a group, it must also be possessed by any particular member of that group. If anyone is not prepared to accept the truth of this conclusion, it is difficult to see what kind of proof could be devised which would be convincing. There are certain basic principles the truth of which must be accepted, for the simple reason that it is not possible to find any principle which is more obviously true and, unless we are prepared to accept some things as being obviously true, there can be no possibility of building any kind of logical structure. Logic itself is the science of reasoning, and we should be reasoning in a circle if we attempted to establish the truth of basic logical principles by using these same basic logical principles. If we are not prepared to accept, for example, that, if a certain statement is true, the statement which contradicts it cannot also be true, then we can make no progress.

If you want to make any progress in geometry, you must be prepared to accept the fundamental axioms. You must agree that a straight line is the shortest distance between two points, or you will never advance to prove the theorem of Pythagoras. Bertrand Russell says that when he first studied geometry, he was very disillusioned to discover that the axioms had to be taken for granted, but he soon realized that he had no alternative.

The statements about Mr. Smith and all bald men can be arranged in such a way as to form one of the commonest types of logical argument, called a 'syllogism'.

a. All bald men make bad husbands.
b. Mr. Smith is bald.
c. Mr. Smith will make a bad husband.

The statement *a* is called the 'major premise', *b* the 'minor premise', and *c* the 'conclusion'. If, as in the above example, the relationship between the premises and the conclusion is such that we are justified in inferring the one from the others, then we say that the argument is 'valid'. If the inference is not justified, then the argument is 'invalid'.

At this stage, it is important to point out that deductive arguments are concerned solely with the relationship between the premises and the conclusion; they are not concerned with the truth of either. It is not true that all bald men make bad husbands, so we cannot use this to prove that Mr. Smith will make a bad husband. The argument as expressed is a valid one, but from the validity of the argument we can tell nothing about the truth of either the premises or the conclusion. If the major premise of an argument is false, we cannot tell whether the conclusion is true or false; Mr. Smith may or may not make a bad husband.

Consider the two statements:

1. A is larger than B.
2. B is larger than C.

If we look upon them as the premises of an argument, we can see that we are justified in arriving at the conclusion

3. A is larger than C.

If the premises 1 and 2 are true, then the conclusion 3 must also be true. We can ask anyone who doubts or denies the validity of the argument to think again, but there is nothing else we can do to show him that he is wrong.

In the same way, if 'All A are B' and 'All C are A', it must follow that 'All C are B'. When we substitute objects and qualities for the letters, we get an argument of the following kind:

1. All men are animals.
2. All bachelors are men.
3. All bachelors are animals.

All arguments of this form are valid.

The premises and conclusion of a syllogism are categorical statements, each of which is made up of a subject and a predicate, called 'terms'.

Thus, in the syllogism:

1. All motor cars are vehicles.
2. All vehicles have wheels.
3. All motor cars have wheels.

'motor cars' is the subject term, and 'vehicles' the predicate term, of the major premises. In the minor premise, 'vehicles' becomes the subject term and 'wheels' is the predicate term. Altogether, we have three terms, 'vehicles' appearing in both the major and minor premises. The term 'vehicles', which is common to both premises, is called the middle term, and it is because of this common term that we can deduce a valid conclusion. If we had premises with four terms, and thus no common term, we could deduce nothing at all. For example, we can make no deduction from the premises:

1. All motor cars are vehicles.
2. All bicycles have wheels.

The two statements, being completely unrelated to one another, give no grounds for reaching any conclusion. The validity of an argument depends on the way the terms are arranged in the premises and the conclusion, and a detailed study of logic provides very precise rules for deciding whether an argument is valid or invalid.

It will be sufficient for us to study a few examples of syllogistic reasoning, and to note some of the common fallacies which arise.

1. All soldiers are brave.
2. Some soldiers are Frenchmen.
3. Some Frenchmen are brave.

This syllogism is clearly valid. But if we change the 'all' of the first premise to 'some', we get:

1. Some soldiers are brave.
2. Some soldiers are Frenchmen.
3. Some Frenchmen are brave.

It is certainly true that some Frenchmen are brave, but we cannot deduce it from the premises of this syllogism. The 'some soldiers' of the first premise, who are brave, may be quite different people from the 'some soldiers' of the second premise, who are Frenchmen. There is no middle term which is common to both premises and consequently no conclusion can be drawn from them. Because the 'some soldiers' of the major premise are not necessarily the 'some soldiers' of the minor premise, we have a syllogism with four terms, from which nothing can be deduced. What may appear to be a middle term is not in fact 'distributed' between the two premises, and the resulting invalid argument is called the 'fallacy of the undistributed middle'.

If, in a political argument, someone says 'Only those who are patriotic vote Conservative', he no doubt wishes to imply that the person with whom he is arguing, and who presumably does not vote Conservative, is not patriotic. But even if his statement is true, this implication does not follow from it. What he is saying is that all those who vote Conservative are patriotic, not that all those who are patriotic vote Conservative. This is again the 'fallacy of the undistributed middle'. To say 'Only those who are patriotic vote Conservative' does not say anything about the whole class of patriotic people, but only about that section of the class who vote Conservative.

Susan Stebbing, in *Thinking to some Purpose*, gives a good example of this same logical fallacy.

'His generosity might have been inferred from his humanity, for all generous people are humane.' This is an argument of the form:

> All A are B.
> All C are B.
> ∴ All C are A.

which, as we have already seen, is invalid. 'All generous people are humane' does not necessarily imply that only generous people are humane or that all humane people are generous. There may be humane people who are not included in the B of the first premise, and C may be some of these—hence C may not be generous. B, the middle term of the syllogism, is not distributed.

In an argument, we seldom find that the premises and conclusion are stated in the precise form of the syllogism. The conclusion is sometimes given before the premises, and quite often one of the premises is not explicitly stated but taken for granted. For example, 'You can vote because you are over 21' can be arranged as a syllogism if we supply the missing premise.

> All people over 21 can vote.
> You are over 21.
> Therefore You can vote.

One of the most important practical rules in criticizing arguments is to make explicit all the assumptions which have not been stated but which are necessary if the argument is to be valid.

3. HYPOTHETICAL ARGUMENTS

We have already seen that statements of the form 'If . . . then . . .' are called hypothetical, and that the 'If . . .' clause is the antecedent and the 'then . . .' clause the consequent. We have also noted that the relationship between the antecedent and the consequent may be deductive, as in: 'If Smith is a novelist, then he is a writer', or inductive, as in 'If you don't wear a hat, you will catch a cold.' In both these hypothetical statements, in order that the consequents may be true, it is sufficient that the antecedents are true, but the degree of truth is not the same in them both. The deductive hypothetical statement, if true, is necessarily true, whereas the inductive statement is only probably true. To make sure he fully understands this important distinction the reader is advised to read again the relevant sections on page 28.

Sufficient and Necessary Conditions

In the hypothetical statement 'If Smith is a novelist, then he is a writer', although it is sufficient for Smith to be a novelist in order to be a writer, it is quite clear that he can be a writer without being a novelist. If he were a dramatist or a poet he would still be a writer. That is, being a novelist is a sufficient condition for being a writer, but not a necessary one. In the same way, although not wearing a hat may be quite enough to make me catch cold, failing to wear a pullover may just as surely achieve the same result. We can put it another way by saying that not wearing a hat may be a sufficient condition for catching a cold, but it is not a necessary one.

Sometimes the antecedent of a hypothetical statement does express both a sufficient and a necessary condition of the consequent. Consider the example 'If yesterday was Friday, then today is Saturday.' We notice that not only is it sufficient for yesterday to have been Friday in order that today shall be Saturday, but it is also necessary that it should have been. Today cannot be Saturday without yesterday having been Friday. We can rewrite the statement as 'If, and only if, yesterday was Friday is today Saturday.' By adding the words 'only if', which exclude all the other days of the week, we are indicating that the antecedent is a necessary as well as a sufficient condition of the consequent.

The above is an example of a deductive hypothetical statement, but the same applies to hypothetical statements when they are inductive. In the statement 'If you work hard, you will pass your examination', the antecedent is a sufficient condition for the truth of the consequent (it has to be a sufficient condition, otherwise it would not be true), but it is not a necessary condition. It does not exclude the possibility of passing the examination without working hard. We can, however, exclude this possibility, thus making the condition both sufficient and necessary, by adding the words 'only if'. 'If, and only if, you work hard will you pass your examination' lays down both a sufficient and necessary condition.

Failure to distinguish between conditions which are both sufficient and necessary and those which are merely sufficient can often lead to faulty reasoning, and hence to false conclusions, as we shall see when we discuss hypothetical arguments.

(a) Affirming the Antecedent

'If I eat green apples, then I shall be ill' is a hypothetical statement, but not yet a hypothetical argument. To turn the statement into an argument, we need to refer it to an actual situation by a factual premise indicating whether or not I do eat the apples, which in its turn will lead to an explicitly stated conclusion. Thus a full hypothetical argument would be as follows:

> If I eat green apples, then I shall be ill.
> I eat green apples.
> Therefore I shall be ill.

It is quite obvious that if the first two statements, or premises, are true, then the conclusion must also be true. But not only is this conclusion true, the conclusion of all arguments of this form is also true.

We can see more clearly the precise form of the argument if we substitute symbols for the statements used. In the above argument, there are two statements 'I eat green apples' and 'I am ill', and if we put the letter 'p' for the first of these and the letter 'q' for the second, we can rewrite the argument as:

> If p, then q.
> p.
> $\therefore q$.

39

Whatever statements we substitute for the p and q of the argument, if the premises are true the conclusion is bound to be true because the form is valid. If the premises are false, then the conclusion will be false.

We have already said that in order to turn a hypothetical statement into a hypothetical argument we need a factual premise. In the argument set out above, we obtained this second premise by stating that the 'If . . .', or antecedent, part of the first premise, is actually the case. We stated, or affirmed, that I did eat the apples. All hypothetical arguments of this form are known as 'affirming the antecedent', and they are all valid.

(b) Affirming the Consequent

If the reasoning in an argument is invalid, then there is no connection between the truth or falsity of the premises and the truth or falsity of the conclusion. We may have invalid reasoning from true premises and yet arrive at a conclusion which is true. For example:

> If Smith is a novelist, then he is a writer.
> Smith is a writer.
> Therefore Smith is a novelist.

It is true that, if Smith is a novelist, he is also a writer. But from this true premise and the fact that Smith is a writer we cannot deduce that he is a novelist, although it may be perfectly true that he is one. This is an invalid argument from true premises to a possibly true conclusion. It is not uncommon for people to reach the right conclusion for the wrong reasons.

This type of argument can be expressed in symbols as:

> If p, then q.
> q.
> $\therefore p$.

Any argument of this form, whatever statements we substitute for p and q, is invalid. In the second premise we affirm q, which is the consequent of the first premise; hence this form of argument is called, 'affirming the consequent'. All arguments which involve affirming the consequent are invalid.

Here is another example:

If you work hard, you will pass your examination.
You have passed your examination.
Therefore you must have worked hard.

The initial premise merely states that working hard is a sufficient condition for passing the examination, not that it is a necessary one. You may have passed the examination even though you did not work hard. It could be turned into a valid argument by putting in the words 'only if'—'If, and only if, you work hard will you pass your examination.' By doing this we have made the condition both sufficient and necessary.

'Affirming the consequent' is an invalid form of argument, because if p is no more than a sufficient condition for q, which is what we mean when we say 'If p, then q', then q is not a sufficient condition for p. It is only if p is a necessary condition for q that q can be a sufficient condition for p. Nevertheless, whenever p is a sufficient condition for q, q is a necessary condition for p. We can see that this is true from the following example:

'If Jones keeps wicket, he is a cricketer.'

This is true because keeping wicket is a sufficient condition for being a cricketer, but it is not a necessary one. It is not true, however, to say 'If Jones is a cricketer, he is a wicket-keeper', because in order to be a wicket-keeper it is not sufficient to be a cricketer: one can be a cricketer and a bowler. Nevertheless, although it is not sufficient to be a cricketer in order to be a wicket-keeper, it is necessary to be one. One cannot be a wicket-keeper without being a cricketer.

We can express all this in symbols by saying: 'If p, then q.' For this to be true, p must be a sufficient condition for q, and from it we can infer that q is a necessary condition for p. We can see that this must be true because it is impossible to have p without also having q. But having q does not mean that we must also have p, because q is not a sufficient condition for p.

(c) Denying the Consequent

Consider the example:

If you press this button, the bell will ring.
The bell does not ring.
Therefore you did not press the button.

The form of the argument is:

> If p, then q.
> Not q.
> ∴ Not p.

This form of argument, which is called 'denying the consequent', is clearly a valid one.

If the consequent of the first premise is a negative statement, then a denial of the consequent will give us an affirmative for the second premise. For example:

> If you take these pills, you will not be sea-sick.
> You are sea-sick.
> Therefore you did not take these pills.

or:

> If p, then not q.
> q.
> ∴ Not p.

(d) Denying the Antecedent

Denying the consequent, as we have just seen, is a valid form of argument, but we must be careful not to confuse this with denying the antecedent, which is an invalid form. For example:

> If John did this work by himself, then he is a very clever boy.
> He did not do it by himself.
> Therefore he is not a clever boy.

If John did the work by himself, this would be a sufficient condition for calling him a clever boy, but he could still be a clever boy even though he did not do the work by himself. That is, doing the work by himself is not a necessary condition of his being a clever boy.

An argument of the form:

> If p, then q.
> Not p.
> ∴ Not q.

is therefore invalid. It would be valid only if p were also a necessary condition for q.

Here is another example of the fallacy of 'denying the antecedent'.

> If he is a Socialist, he believes in nationalization.
> He is not a Socialist.
> Therefore he does not believe in nationalization.

Being a Socialist is a sufficient condition for believing in nationalization, but it is not a necessary one. One can be a Conservative, because one rejects all other socialist beliefs, and still be a believer in nationalization.

If we were to say 'If, and only if, he is a Socialist does he believe in nationalization', we should be making 'being a Socialist' into a necessary condition for believing in nationalization, and a belief in nationalization a sufficient condition for being a Socialist. From this it would follow that the Conservative who said he believed in nationalization would, in fact, be a Socialist.

Whenever an antecedent is both a sufficient and a necessary condition for a consequent, we can both affirm the consequent and deny the antecedent and still have a valid form of argument. This can be seen from the following example: 'If a figure has three equal angles, it is an equilateral triangle.' It is also true to say that if it is an equilateral triangle, it has three equal angles, and if it does not have three equal angles it is not an equilateral triangle.

4. THE DILEMMA

It must not be thought that an understanding of the various forms of deductive reasoning we have been discussing is of value only if we wish to detect the fallacies in the arguments of other people. Even if we are not argumentatively inclined, we cannot avoid the necessity of arguing with ourselves if we wish to hold reasonable beliefs and to behave as fully rational human beings. We are constantly being faced with choices between different courses of action, one of which must be chosen and the others rejected. When we find these choices particularly difficult, we sometimes say we are in a dilemma. Thus, a conscientious elector may argue with himself as follows: 'If I vote Socialist, taxes will go up; and if I vote Conservative, unemployment will rise. But I have to vote

Socialist or Conservative; therefore, either taxes or unemployment will go up.' The elector seems to be presented with two possible courses of action, both of which seem undesirable; this is the situation we call a dilemma.

We can express his argument in the following form:

If p, then q and if r, then s.
Either p or r.
$\therefore$ q or s.

This is a complex version of the hypothetical argument, presenting us with alternative conclusions, both of which are unpalatable. Because of its complexity, it is not always easy to see a way out of a dilemma, and consequently it is a device which speakers frequently use to persuade, and sometimes to deceive.

The two hypothetical statements of the main premise of a dilemma are sometimes referred to as 'horns', and when the dilemma is a real one, we find ourselves in the unpleasant situation of being impaled on one or other of these horns. All dilemmas, however, are not as real as they often appear at first sight, and there are two main ways of avoiding their painful consequences.

(a) 'Slipping Between the Horns'

The first way is to find a third path which will enable us to slip, as it were, between the horns: we may avoid being caught on either of the sharp horns by finding a way between them. In order to do this, we have to show that the alternatives presented are not real alternatives. Let us look at the following dilemma:

If John is clever, he doesn't need teachers and if he is stupid, he cannot profit by them.
He is either stupid or clever.
Therefore it is no use for John to have teachers.

But John need not be either stupid or clever. Because a person is not stupid it does not follow that he must be clever, nor is he necessarily stupid if he is not clever—most people fall somewhere between the two extremes. As soon as we realize that John may be of average intelligence, the dilemma ceases to exist—we have slipped between its horns.

44

(b) 'Taking the Dilemma by the Horns'

The second way is to deny that the horns really are horns; in other words, to deny that one of the hypothetical statements of the major premise is true. For example:

Either you get a job or you do not.
If you get a job you will be tired and unhappy, and if you do not you will be bored and miserable.
Therefore you will be either tired and unhappy or bored and miserable.

There is no way of slipping between the horns of this dilemma; you must either get a job or not get a job. But we do not have to accept the truth of either of the statements in the major premise. It is not necessarily true that we shall be tired and unhappy if we start to work, or bored and miserable if we do not get a job but stay at home. We have seized the dilemma by the horns by challenging the truth of both its hypothetical statements.

FOR DISCUSSION AND ESSAYS

1. Consider whether the following arguments are valid or invalid. Give reasons.
    a. It is a good thing to open betting shops because it shows enterprise, and it is good to show enterprise.
    b. If he had left home at 7 a.m. he would have caught the train. But I know that he was still at home at 7.5 a.m., so he must have missed it.
    c. He doesn't bathe unless the sun is shining, and seeing that the sun is not shining now he won't be bathing.
    d. If I drink and drive I am a danger on the road and if I don't drink I feel miserable. So I have to choose between feeling miserable and driving dangerously.
    e. Homosexuality is a wrongful sexual act and so is adultery. This goes to show that homosexuality is really nothing less than adultery.
    f. Whenever there is snow there are more accidents, so it must have snowed last week to account for the rise in the number of accidents.

 g. Only people who have a social conscience vote Labour, so you can't have a social conscience if you vote Conservative.

 h. He always rings me up if he misses the train. He hasn't rung me, so he must have caught it.

 i. He won't need your help if he is hardworking, and if he is lazy he won't profit by it. So there is no point in helping him.

 j. 'He says he isn't going out if he feels tired.'
  'He has just said he is going out.'
  'He can't feel tired then.'

2. Criticize the following hypothetical syllogisms, stating whether or not each one is valid.

 a. If a man is innocent he should not be punished. This man should not be punished; therefore he is innocent.

 b. If a man does not believe the Bible, he is unorthodox. But since you do believe the Bible, it follows that you are orthodox.

 c. If the government is just, the rights of no one will be exploited. But under the present government the rights of some people are exploited. Therefore the present government is not a just one.

3. What two conditions are necessary before we can be sure that the conclusion of a deductive argument is true?

CHAPTER 3

INDUCTION

I. VALIDITY AND TRUTH

To reason deductively is to draw a conclusion from given premises. From the premises

> All men are mortal.
> Socrates is a man.

we can deduce that Socrates is mortal. When the reasoning is correct, we say that it is valid, when incorrect it is invalid. However, to say that the conclusion is the result of a valid argument does not mean that it is also a true conclusion. The truth of a conclusion does not depend only on the validity of the argument. Before the conclusion can be true, it must be validly deduced from true premises, but we cannot apply the same tests for the truth of a premise as for the validity of an argument. What we have been considering so far is how we know a deductive argument to be valid; we must now try to decide how we know when a premise is true.

It is the premise which gives us information; the process of deduction merely explores the relationship between various premises and gives us no new facts. The following is a valid syllogism:

> All men are mortal.
> Socrates is a man.
> Therefore Socrates is mortal.

From the two premises we have inferred that Socrates is mortal, but we must have known this as soon as we stated the first premise 'All men are mortal'. If we really know that all men are mortal, we must of course know that Socrates is mortal. There doesn't seem much point in going to the trouble of writing out a syllogism to tell us something we already know. In a sense, this criticism applies to all deductive reasoning: the information which the conclusion supplies is already there in the premises. This is obviously

47

true of the simple syllogism we have quoted above, but it is also true of more complicated deductive reasoning.

Mathematics is a system of deductive inferences from a number of accepted axioms. The theorems of Euclid, for example, illustrate this sort of reasoning, although it would hardly be true to say that we know the theorems provided we know the axioms. Nevertheless, the conclusion of a syllogism is already contained in the premises with which we begin. The study of logic, just like the study of mathematics, brings out the full implications of the knowledge with which we start.

The next thing to consider is how we obtain this primary knowledge which is essential before we can begin any kind of deductive argument. The truth of the syllogism:

> All men are mortal.
> Socrates is a man.
> Therefore Socrates is mortal.

depends on the truth of the two premises. The minor premise 'Socrates is a man' presents little difficulty; it is a simple fact of observation and, in so far as we can be sure of the truth of any statement about the world, we can be sure of it. But the major premise 'All men are mortal' cannot be verified in such a straightforward way; it is not a simple fact of observation. We can feel more sure of the truth of the conclusion 'Socrates is mortal' than of the premise 'All men are mortal'. It is just because we know that particular individuals are mortal that we conclude that all men are mortal. But are we justified in assuming that because X, Y and Z are mortal, therefore all men are mortal?

We frequently use general statements of the kind 'If you place wood in the fire, it will burn' as a premise for a deductive argument. Thus we may argue as follows:

> If you place wood in the fire, it will burn.
> This is a piece of wood.
> Therefore this will burn.

But how do we know that the major premise is true? We have placed several pieces of wood in the fire in the past, and in every case the wood has burned. We make the assumption that it will do so in the future. But on what grounds?

The process by which we generalize from a number of cases of which something is true, and infer that the same thing is true of all members of the same class, is called induction. We are reasoning inductively when we conclude that wood will burn on the grounds that it always has done. From what has happened to all the pieces of wood we have examined, we infer that the same thing will happen to all the pieces of wood we have not examined.

Inductive reasoning thus involves a leap from the known to the unknown, and in this respect differs from deductive reasoning, which merely brings out into the open what, in a sense, we know already. How we can justify this inductive jump has puzzled philosophers for many centuries, and is known as the 'problem of induction'.

If I were to say, 'Prior to 1939 all English cricket captains were amateurs', I should be making a generalization, but it would be based upon an exhaustive knowledge of all the English captains. It would not be inductive reasoning, because it makes no jump from the known to the unknown.

On the other hand, if I pick at random five potatoes from a sack and find them rotten, and if I infer from this that all the potatoes in the sack are rotten, I am reasoning inductively, because I am making a jump from the known to the unknown. Assuming there are a hundred potatoes in the sack and I find that ninety-nine of them are rotten, am I justified in inferring that the hundredth potato will also be rotten? No doubt we shall feel certain that it will be, but the certainty will be in our own minds and not in the inference itself. From the statement 'All the potatoes examined are rotten' we cannot logically infer 'All the potatoes in the sack are rotten.' This is not a valid deductive argument, because we cannot deduce anything about all potatoes from knowledge about some potatoes.

Nevertheless, our knowledge about matters of fact would be very limited if we were unable to reach conclusions beyond what we discover immediately from our senses. I can observe a piece of wood burning in the fire, but unless it is possible to make a generalization from this immediate observation, I cannot say anything about how wood will behave on future occasions if placed on the fire. We all assume that we are justified in making such generalizations, but we cannot decide whether they are true by the criteria which are used in deductive arguments. The truth of inductive arguments depends on the amount and kind of evidence we can produce in support, and so it follows that the degree of trust we can put in inductive conclusions will vary considerably from one to another.

2. INDUCTION BY SIMPLE ENUMERATION

If all the Spaniards I know are dark, I may be tempted to generalize from this knowledge and say that all Spaniards are dark; but such a conclusion will be shown to be untrue as soon as I meet a Spaniard who is not dark. This form of inductive argument, in which conclusions are drawn about all the members of a class from observation about some members of that class, is called 'induction by simple enumeration'. Although my conclusion about all Spaniards is proved to be untrue as soon as I meet one who is not dark, I do not have to abandon my generalization, but can modify it to fit the facts. I cannot truthfully say that all Spaniards are dark, but I may still be able to make a useful generalization and say that most Spaniards are dark.

The precision and accuracy of our inductive conclusions depend on the precision and accuracy of the supporting evidence. If, from a bag of peas, I take a large handful and, on examination, find that three-quarters of them are worm-eaten, I may well be justified in concluding that three-quarters of the peas in the bag are worm-eaten. This method of random sampling is the basis of the technique used in the various opinion polls. A pollster may ask 2000 Conservatives whether they approve of Britain's having a nuclear deterrent, and, if he discovers that 85 per cent of his sample approve, he concludes that 85 per cent of all Conservatives also approve. There are, however, certain possible sources of error in induction by simple enumeration, and the reliability of our conclusions will depend on whether or not we have guarded against them.

(a) Insufficient Evidence

The most common source of error is insufficient evidence. We cannot expect to reach a reliable conclusion about the peas in a bag if we examine only half a dozen, and we cannot be absolutely certain what all the peas are like without examining them all. But somewhere between examining half a dozen, when no satisfactory conclusion is possible, and examining all, when certainty is attained, there is a number which will give us reasonably reliable information about all the peas. If the pollster questions only 20 conservatives about their attitude to nuclear weapons, he may get a result which is greatly at variance with the opinion of most Conservatives. But it is impossible to say exactly how many peas must be examined, or how many conservatives must be questioned, before we can reach a reliable conclusion; such knowledge can be derived only from experience in the particular field of enquiry.

Most of our knowledge about everyday things is derived from induction by simple enumeration, and this is the way primitive man began to understand his environment. When he appeased his hunger by eating berries, or quenched his thirst by drinking water, it was as a result of inductive generalizations. In the same way most of our superstitions and prejudices are the result of making generalizations, but on insufficient evidence. For example, the Englishman who goes abroad and meets a handful of foreigners who are inconsiderate and aggressive may think he is justified in concluding that all foreigners are the same. We have all met the person who argues that because old Mr. Smith is ninety and has smoked cigarettes all his life, there cannot be any danger in smoking; or the one who says that 'X' television sets are inferior because his neighbour has had a lot of trouble with his.

In all forms of induction by simple enumeration, we must avoid, on the one hand, hasty generalizations from insufficient evidence and, on the other, refusal to accept conclusions even when there is a reasonable amount of evidence.

(b) Avoidance of Bias

When we make a generalization about all the members of a class or group from an examination of a relatively small number of members, we must ensure that our sample is not biased in any way. If we assume that all the peas in a bag are rotten because we find that all those in a handful we take from the top are rotten, we may be making a very bad mistake. The top layer of peas may have been exposed to conditions which caused them to go rotten, while all the rest of the peas are perfectly sound. Before it is safe to generalize about all the peas from a chosen handful, it is essential to see that all the peas are so completely mixed that there is no variation in different parts of the bag.

The experts who publish public opinion polls cannot mix up the inhabitants of a country, as they would peas in a bag, in order to obtain a representative sample; they have to use much more sophisticated methods to achieve the same result. On any political or social issue, opinions vary considerably according to occupation, education, locality, wealth and various other factors, so that, in order to reach a true picture of the state of public opinion, it is necessary to take account of all these factors. The sampling must be done in such a way that each one of them is given its due weight.

We are all inclined at one time or another to make generalizations which are based on a biased selection of evidence. We may have been justified in forming the belief that a certain rugby team plays a dirty game, but once we believe this to be true there is a strong tendency to look for evidence which will support the belief and to ignore all the evidence against it. We like to cling to our beliefs as long as we can, and find it difficult to give the proper weight to evidence which might make us change them.

Many of our superstitions survive because of this biased selection of evidence, as Francis Bacon observed: 'The human understanding when it has once adopted an opinion (either as being the received opinion or as being agreeable to itself) draws all things else to support and agree with it. And though there be a greater number and weight of instances to be found on the other side, yet these it either neglects and despises, or else by some distinction sets aside and rejects; in order that by this great and pernicious predetermination the authority of its former conclusions may remain inviolate. And therefore it was a good answer that was made by one who, when they showed him hanging in a temple a picture of those who had paid their vows as having escaped shipwreck, and would have him say whether he did now acknowledge the power of the gods,—"Aye", asked he again, "but where are they painted that were drowned after their vows?" And such is the way of all superstition, whether in astrology, dreams, omens, divine judgements, or the like, wherein men, having a delight in such vanities, mark the events where they are fulfilled, but where they fail, though this happens much oftener, neglect and pass them by.'

The biased selection of evidence to support certain beliefs is often found in times of great stress. During the bombing raids of the last war, when it happened that someone's life was saved by a strange combination of circumstances, the fact was sometimes produced as evidence for the belief that a superior power was protecting our war effort. This belief was in no way weakened by all those occasions when lives were lost. The belief that God protected our troops during the evacuation from Dunkirk took no account of all the military reverses which led to that desperate situation. We can preserve any belief if we are prepared to select our evidence in this way.

3. CAUSAL INDUCTION

If we select at random six pupils from a class of thirty, and discover that their knowledge of mathematics is below average, we may conclude that the standard of the whole class is below average. This conclusion would be arrived at by a process of simple enumeration, and would be more reliable if we selected a further six pupils and found the same result. We might then begin to wonder about the reason for this state of affairs and, if we discovered that the class had had no mathematics teacher for twelve months, we should feel even more sure that our generalization about the mathematical ability of the class as a whole was justified. Once we had discovered a causal explanation of the situation, we could have much more confidence in our inference.

The evidence for the belief that cigarette smoking is one of the causes of lung cancer is very strong, but it is based upon induction by simple enumeration. The more evidence of this kind that can be collected, the more certain does the inference become, but a direct causal link between cigarette smoking and lung cancer would be even more convincing.

Much of our understanding of our environment is the result of the discovery of such causal connections. When we place a piece of wood on the fire, we say that it is the fire which causes the wood to burn, and we believe that the same cause will produce the same effect in the future. We assume that nature behaves in a uniform manner, but are we justified in making such an assumption? From our everyday experience of life, it would certainly seem that we are; we find that the food which satisfied our hunger yesterday continues to satisfy it today, that water has lost none of its power to quench our thirst. If we drop things, they fall to the ground, as they have always done in the past. Such apparent regularity most certainly conditions us to believe in the uniformity of nature, but to explain why we have this belief is not the same as to justify it.

We could justify our belief in the regularity of particular events if only there were some means of knowing that nature behaves uniformly. We could use this fact as a major premise, and reach conclusions about particular events by a process of deduction. We could indicate the uniformity of nature by saying 'Like causes produce like effects' and obtain the following deductive argument:

Like causes produce like effects.
Heat has always melted snow.
Therefore this heat will melt this snow.

If the major premise could be known to be certainly true, then the conclusion would also be certainly true. We should have succeeded in turning an inductive argument into a deductive one, and in the process achieved the certainty which goes with deduction. But the problem still remains of how we establish the truth of the major premise 'Like causes produce like effects'. If we say that we know that nature is uniform because always in the past like causes have produced like effects, we cannot go on to argue that like causes will produce like effects because of the uniformity of nature. This would be arguing in a circle: assuming to be true that which we set out to prove. There is, in fact, no way of turning an inductive into a deductive argument; we can assume the uniformity, but we cannot prove our assumption.

Hume, the distinguished eighteenth-century philosopher, was the first to state explicitly what was required for a Principle of Induction. He wrote: 'Instances, of which we have had no experience, must resemble those, of which we have had experience, and . . . the course of nature continues always uniformly the same.' He himself, however, remained sceptical and wrote: 'If we believe that

54

fire warms, or water refreshes, 'tis only because it costs us too much pains to think otherwise.'

Although we can give no logical reason for the assumption that nature is uniform, it would seem very misguided to think otherwise. If we desire to exert any control over our environment, we are bound to make this assumption, though we must also be prepared to admit that by doing so we are begging the whole question.

4. THE QUEST FOR CERTAINTY

The two processes of reasoning, deduction and induction, are the two ways we have of understanding the world. Induction, which is based on observation, and deduction, based on thinking about our observations.

The ancients believed that the kind of knowledge obtained from thought was more reliable and essentially superior to that obtained by observation—our senses may deceive us, we suffer from hallucinations, and often things are not what they seem. The stick in the water looks bent, but we believe that 'really' it is straight; the pool of water in the desert is not an oasis, but an optical illusion. Pure thought, or reason, as exemplified in the process of deduction, does not lead us astray in this way, and when we reach a deductive conclusion we can be certain of its truth. Such certainty is not to be found in inductive reasoning: there is no inevitability about our observations of the world, or in any generalizations we make from them. We can be certain that two and two make four, at all times and under all conditions, but, although we have always observed in the past that heat melts snow, we cannot be certain that it always will in the future.

For these reasons, from fifth-century Athens to seventeenth-century England, deduction was considered superior to induction, and the only way of obtaining true knowledge. Descartes, the seventeenth-century French philosopher, although he was determined to break with all the traditional ideas of the past, thought that deduction was the only reliable method to use. He wanted to place all our knowledge on a sure foundation, and he thought that this could best be done by doubting everything and beginning again from first principles. He came to the conclusion that the only things of which he could be absolutely certain were his own existence and the existence of God. He could not doubt that he was thinking, and if he was thinking it must follow that he was also existing. But his own existence was not sufficient by itself to enable him to be sure of any knowledge about the world around him. We often suffer from illusions and hallucinations about reality and, if this is so, how can we be certain that our senses do not always deceive us?

Descartes believed that certainty about our knowledge of the external world is possible only on the assumption that there is a righteous God who would not have created man in order to deceive him in this way. He thought that we are justified in our belief that we have bodies and that there are objects in space only because there is a God in whom we can put our trust.

It was from these two certainties—his own existence and that of God—that Descartes thought he could deduce all knowledge about the universe, and with the certainty we find in a geometrical theorem. He was not interested in observation and experiment, for the only information to be obtained in this way is not certain, and certainty was the one thing that Descartes demanded. In practice, what he did was to take knowledge that had been obtained empirically, and then try to show how it could be deduced from the existence of God; but by this method of deduction he could not discover any new facts about the universe.

Although we now know that deduction does not give us knowledge about the world, the philosophy of Descartes, with its quest for certainty, still influences philosophical thought, especially on the continent of Europe. The existentialists, whose theories can best be studied in the works of Sartre, are, like Descartes, dissatisfied with the uncertainty of empirical knowledge but, unlike Descartes, they realize that any search for certainty is a vain one. The world is as we find it, but there is no necessity in its being as it is; it might have been different. The laws of nature are not rules of logic, and we cannot deduce what the world is like from self-evident truths.

Such an inescapable conclusion causes the existentialist to look upon human life as absurd—absurd because it is devoid of logical sense. He longs to discover some necessity in things and events, and when he finds that he cannot, because the world is not a deductive system, he feels the situation to be intolerable. It is the realization that induction does not lead to necessary truths that produces the 'nausea' which plays such an important part in the philosophy of Sartre and the existentialists.

5. SCIENTIFIC METHOD

(a) *Induction replaces Deduction*

The discoveries of science have had such a profound effect on all our lives that it is difficult for us to realize that the modern scientific age is only three or four hundred years old. There were scientists in ancient Greece more than two thousand years ago, men like Democritus, who put forward an atomic theory, and Archimedes, who discovered the principle of the lever, but their teaching and methods exerted practically no influence on later thought. Their scientific approach, based on observation and experiment and therefore inductive, was rejected in favour of the deductive approach of Plato and Aristotle. If Democritus and Archimedes had survived and Plato and Aristotle had been discarded, the effect on the course of history would have been enormous; but the Greek scientists were forgotten and for two thousand years science ceased to exist.

The person most responsible for this almost total eclipse of the scientific spirit was Aristotle. Like Plato, he believed that true knowledge, knowledge which can be *proved* to be true, can be obtained only by deduction. But, as we have already seen, the truth of the conclusion of a deductive argument cannot be more certain than the truth of the premises, and if the premises are based on observation and experiment, then the conclusion can be only inductively true. The only way we can reach a conclusion which has the deductive truth which Aristotle demanded is to derive it from premises which are themselves deductively true. This kind of reasoning, however, involves us in what the philosopher calls an 'infinite regress'; there must be some point at which we stop and say that there are premises which are known to be certainly true without deducing them from other premises.

Aristotle believed that there are such premises, he called them 'basic premises', which are not based on ordinary observation but from which all our knowledge of the world can be deduced. He thought that these 'basic premises' are to be discovered by a special power of intuition completely divorced from our ordinary sense perceptions. One such premise is that the world was created by a perfect God. From this we can deduce, according to Aristotle, that the heavenly bodies must move in a perfect orbit, which is a circle. No observation is required to reach this conclusion, and indeed if the conclusion were dependent on observation, it would not be reliable enough to satisfy Aristotle's criterion of true knowledge. Inductive knowledge is uncertain and liable to error; deductive knowledge alone is certain and true. The result was that when Kepler showed that the planets move in ellipses, and not in circles, his conclusions were rejected because they conflicted with those which were reached deductively.

Behind the many clashes between the deductive and inductive approaches to knowledge which we find in the sixteenth and seventeenth centuries there lie the figure of Aristotle and the authority of the Bible. Whatever evidence Copernicus, Kepler or Galileo might bring for their revolutionary theories, they were rejected out of hand if they did not agree with what Aristotle and the Bible said. The medieval attitude was that truth was something which was known in the past and could be found again by consulting that past; it was not something which could go on increasing and be discovered by the unfettered and freely enquiring mind.

It is written in the Psalms 'The world also is established, that it cannot be moved', and Calvin used this text to refute Copernicus' revolutionary theory that the earth moves. 'Who will venture', he wrote, 'to place the authority of Copernicus above that of the Holy Spirit?' What Calvin did not realize, however, was that in the new science there are no authorities; it is not a question of Copernicus taking the place of the Holy Spirit, but of observation, or induction, taking the place of deduction.

The authoritarian attitude to knowledge seems very strange to us today, but people who had been brought up to believe that deduction was the only way to true knowledge did not find it as difficult as we should to reject the evidence of the senses. In 1629, Galileo wrote a book entitled *Dialogue Concerning the Two Chief World Systems*, in which he contrasted the Aristotelian and his own scientific approach to knowledge. The difference between them is well illustrated by the following extract: 'One day I was at the home of a very famous doctor in Venice, where many persons came on account of their studies, and others occasionally came out of curiosity to see some anatomical dissection performed by a man who was truly no less learned than he was a careful and expert anatomist. It happened on this day that he was investigating the source and origin of the nerves, about which there exists a notorious controversy between the Galenist and Peripatetic doctors. The anatomist showed that the great trunk of nerves, leaving the brain and passing through the nape, extended on down the spine and then branched out through the whole body, and that only a single strand as fine as a thread arrived at the heart. Turning to a gentleman whom he knew to be a Peripatetic philosopher, and on whose account he had been exhibiting and demonstrating everything with unusual care, he asked this man whether he was at last satisfied and convinced that the nerves originated in the brain and not in the heart. The philosopher, after considering for a while, answered: "You have made me see this matter so plainly and palpably that if Aristotle's text were not contrary to it, stating clearly that the nerves originates in the heart, I should be forced to admit it to be true." ' For the Peripatetic philosopher seeing was not believing, if it contradicted the authority of Aristotle.

We now believe that Aristotle was right to claim that knowledge which is certain can be obtained only by deduction, but wrong to think that such knowledge can be about the world; knowledge of fact can be obtained only by observation, or induction, but it is not certain and cannot be proved to be true. The willingness to accept the limitations of induction, and the awareness that the process of deduction does not lead to new knowledge, were responsible for the advances made in scientific studies. Francis Bacon was one of the first to break clear from the influence of Aristotle, and it was while he was still at Cambridge that, in his own words, he 'first fell into the dislike of the philosophy of Aristotle'. He also realized the importance of replacing deduction by induction, as when he wrote: 'We reject the syllogistic method as being too confused and allowing nature to escape out of our hands. In everything relating to the nature of things we make use of induction for both our major and minor premises.' He saw that the syllogism was not the way to get to grips with nature, and that we must use induction to establish the truth of our premises. Nevertheless, he failed to understand the limitations of induction as a method of obtaining new knowledge, and did not realize that the knowledge so obtained lacked the certainty of deductive inference.

(b) Forming Hypotheses

Bacon assumed that it was possible to use induction as a mechanical process. All we needed to do, he thought, was to observe and let the facts speak for themselves; observation would automatically lead, by the process of induction, to true generalizations. But facts do not speak for themselves; they must be arranged by a speculative mind. Scientific discoveries are made by people searching for answers to puzzles, and success depends on the ability to distinguish the relevant from the irrelevant fact. This ability is the result of a wide knowledge of the field of study: unless we are fully acquainted with what is already known, we cannot be in a position to judge of the relevance of something new. In order to reach an understanding of the facts, we must be able to relate them to one another and see how they fit in with what we already know. To succeed in this, we need the gift of being able to make an imaginative jump from the facts we observe to a general theory, or hypothesis, which will explain them.

Many people before Isaac Newton had seen apples fall from trees, but it was his genius which saw the possible connection between falling apples and the movements of heavenly bodies. As Karl Pearson wrote in his *Grammar of Science*, 'Disciplined imagination has been at the bottom of all great scientific discoveries. All great scientists have in a certain sense been great artists; the man with no imagination may collect facts but he cannot make great discoveries.'

During the seventeenth century, which was a period of transition between the old and the new, the data that scientists collected were both scientific facts and primitive superstitions; they would discuss, almost in the same sentence, the way to discover the weight of air and how to turn base metal into gold. It was only natural that the greater part of the effort expended in scientific work should consist of straightforward observation and the accumulation of facts, for this was the aspect of the new approach to knowledge which most clearly distinguished it from the deductive systems of the past. There were so many things to find out about the world that the purely descriptive aspect of science inevitably took precedence over the search for an explanation of phenomena by general laws.

It is also probably true to say that the imaginative ability needed to formulate hypotheses is much less common than that which is required for observation and experiment. Mrs. Joan Bennett, in her life of Sir Thomas Browne, points out the difference in this respect between Sir Thomas and his son Edward: 'Edward was less imaginative and less speculative than his father, but he had the same impulse to notice and record the facts, and the same excitement, shared with many men of the time, about the gradual accumulation of curious information.'

The birth of modern science would have been impossible if people like Francis Bacon had not realized that induction must take the place of deduction. Understanding of the world must, in the first place, be based upon observation and the collection of what Galileo called 'irreducible and stubborn facts'. Nevertheless, the mere accumulation of facts does not necessarily imply understanding; we need to fit the facts into a pattern and to discover how they illustrate general laws.

Darwin, for example, considered that his own scientific success was founded upon 'industry in observing and collecting facts and a fair share of invention as well as of common sense'. But the facts came first, collected mainly during his explorations of the Galapagos Archipelago. The variations in the different species which he found there, as well as the fossil remains, led him to doubt the common assumption that species were fixed and immutable. He came to the conclusion that, just as breeds of domestic animals and plants can be improved by selection, so there must be a form of selection at work in nature. In their wild state all organisms have to struggle for existence and only those which are best equipped for the struggle survive. Those members of a species best adapted to their environment will have the greatest number of offspring, and the factors which help them to survive will tend to be preserved whereas those factors which have no survival value will eventually be destroyed. In this way the species will gradually evolve.

The theory that organisms have evolved by a process of variation and natural selection not only explains all the known facts; it can also be used in the search for new knowledge. Thus, if there has been an evolution from the more simple to the more complex, then the fossils of the simple organisms will be found in the older strata of rocks and those of the more highly evolved organisms in the newer strata. This prediction, reached deductively from Darwin's theory, has been shown to be correct; the deduction corresponds to the facts and confirms the theory.

Professor P. B. Medawar has written: 'Biology before Darwin was almost all facts . . . there is an epoch in the growth of a science during which facts accumulate faster than theories can accommodate them.' What Darwin did was to change the emphasis in biology from induction to deduction; he moved on from the simple search for more facts to the formulation of a general theory or hypothesis which could serve as a basis for further deductions. In their early stages, all sciences are primarily inductive because they are chiefly concerned with exploring their field of study and collecting purely factual information. As they progress, hypotheses leading to general laws play a greater role, and deduction becomes relatively more important.

(c) Testing Hypotheses

We see, therefore, that induction and deduction both have their part to play in scientific discovery. Out of his knowledge of the facts, the scientist is able to formulate a hypothesis, and from the hypothesis he can deduce other facts which by further observation and experiment he can show to be true or false. He predicts what will happen if his hypothesis is correct, and if his prediction is fulfilled, the hypothesis will be strengthened. It will be verified by each confirmed prediction, and may then reach the status of a scientific law, but it can never be established as true, indubitable and for all time.

This is a characteristic of all scientific hypotheses and laws—they are never more than probably true, as can be seen from the following deductive argument: Let p = the hypothesis, and q, r and s = facts which have been predicted and verified. We then have:

$$\text{If } p, \text{ then } q, r \text{ and } s.$$
$$q, r \text{ and } s.$$
$$\therefore p.$$

This is an invalid form of deductive argument called 'affirming the consequent', and cannot therefore establish the conclusion as being necessarily true. On the other hand, every instance of q, r and s affords some evidence for the truth of p and makes it more probable—but never certain.

Although we can never establish once and for all the truth of a hypothesis, one falsification can destroy it completely. This can also be demonstrated deductively:

> If p, then q, r and s.
> Not q, r and s.
> $\therefore$ Not p.

You will notice that this is deductively valid because it is an example of 'denying the consequent'. If we predict from our hypothesis that certain things will follow and they do not, then it is falsified.

The way in which hypotheses are verified and falsified can be illustrated by a famous example from the history of physics. To explain the motion of light, Newton put forward the hypothesis that light consists of very small particles travelling at enormous speeds. Another scientist, Huygens, thought that a more likely explanation was that it travels in a kind of wave motion. From each of these hypotheses different predictions could be made. From Newton's particle theory, it was possible to deduce that the velocity of light is greater in water than in air, whereas from Huygens' wave theory, the deduction was that the speed is less in water than in air. It was not until 1850, as a result of very great improvements in experimental technique, that Foucault was able to verify Huygens' hypothesis and falsify Newton's.

One of the most dramatic verifications of a prediction in the history of science is afforded by Einstein's theory of general relativity which appeared in 1915. As a part of this theory, Einstein explained that, just as material bodies exert an attraction upon one another, so light is diverted from its path by the attraction of very large bodies, such as the sun. The truth of this gravitational theory was demonstrated by Eddington during a total solar eclipse in 1919. From the observations he made, Eddington was able to show that the light from stars which passed near the sun was deflected in just the way Einstein had predicted.

(d) 'Elementary, my dear Watson'

There is no better way of reaching an understanding of the way scientific discoveries are made than to study the methods of Sherlock Holmes. Although he was inclined to talk about 'deduction', when he should have said 'induction', he provides a good example of the use of both these processes in the solving of the puzzles which were brought to him. Almost any of the stories would serve as illustration, but we will take *The Case of the Six Napoleons*.

Mr. Lestrade, of Scotland Yard, called upon Holmes and gave him the facts of a strange story which had been puzzling the police for some days. A plaster bust of Napoleon, on display in a London shop, had been found smashed on the floor, knocked over apparently by some hooligan who had made good his escape. Three days later, a Dr. Barnicoat, an enthusiastic admirer of Napoleon, returned home to find his house burgled and a plaster cast of Napoleon's head, which he kept in the hall, taken out into the garden and smashed. The doctor had another similar cast in his surgery, and when he went there the next day he found that it too had been broken.

In all, six busts of Napoleon had been made from the same mould, and in the next few days two more of them were stolen and smashed into fragments. This meant that there was only one bust left undamaged.

Holmes rejected Lestrade's hypothesis that it was the work of some maniac who hated the French Emperor, on the grounds that no other statue of him had been damaged. He turned his attention to searching for the sixth bust and it was eventually traced to a Mr. Harding of Reading. When Holmes offered to purchase it for ten pounds, the owner was astonished but willingly agreed to sell. He was even more astonished when Holmes 'picked up his hunting-crop and struck Napoleon a sharp blow on the top of the head'. With a loud shout of triumph, Holmes held up a splinter of the bust in which was embedded a precious black pearl.

From the facts he had discovered, Holmes had formulated the hypothesis that something valuable was hidden in one of the busts, and when he smashed the head and found the pearl, his hypothesis was verified.

The method of Sherlock Holmes, as well as that of the scientist, can be represented as follows:

Facts–Induction–Hypothesis–Deduction–Prediction–Verification–Facts.

A word of explanation is necessary to prevent misunderstanding about the first step of this process: Facts–Induction–Hypothesis. Facts do not automatically lead to a hypothesis; a person may have all the facts and still not be able to make any sense out of them. Sherlock Holmes was a brilliant detective because he was able to select and impose an order on the multitude of things he was told and discovered about a case. He possessed the creative imagination which enabled him to make the jump from facts to hypothesis. This is also true about great scientists; they see a significance in small things which others would ignore.

The inductive relationship between facts and hypothesis merely expresses the grounds for the truth of the hypothesis and not a method of procedure. Scientific hypotheses are inductively true, but they cannot be discovered by a process of induction: they cannot be mechanically derived from facts. We must distinguish between the inductive reasons for believing a hypothesis to be true and the actual way the mind of the scientist works.

Once a hypothesis has been formulated, the scientist can use it to predict what will happen if it is true. This step, from hypothesis to prediction, is purely deductive and one in which logic and mathematics are the chief instruments. Unlike induction, deduction is a mechanical process and requires care and accuracy rather than imaginative powers.

The scientific process is completed when the prediction is either verified or falsified by observation of the facts. We can study this process in action if we look at some of the work which has recently been done on the mental illness known as 'schizophrenia'. The word 'schizophrenia', which means 'split mind', is used to cover a number of mental disorders having certain common characteristics, the most important being disturbed emotional responses and proneness to hallucinations. Schizophrenics may change abruptly from moods of elation to those of deep depression, from laughter to rage; they may also hear imaginary voices from the most unlikely sources.

On the basis of these symptoms, the scientist has to imagine what causal factors are most likely to lie behind them. The most obvious cause of a mental disease might be thought to lie in some stress or conflict between the subject and his environment, but research into the social relationships of schizophrenic patients has failed to produce any really convincing evidence for this. If a hypothesis cannot in any way be substantiated, the only thing to do is to abandon it. This has been done and a completely new approach has been suggested.

There is some evidence that the disease can be passed on from one generation to the next, and this seems to point to a biological rather than a psychological origin. This new hypothesis has opened up a fresh line of enquiry and given research workers a wide field to explore. There have been, inevitably, many false trails. It was thought at first that certain chemicals might be causal factors, because they were found in schizophrenics and not in normal people, but these were subsequently found to be due to the patients' diet or to drugs. However, biological tests revealed that 80 per cent of a certain class of schizophrenics pass in their urine a substance known as D.M.P.E., whereas this is not to be found in the rest of the population. If it were established that this substance is in fact the cause of the disease, there would be high hopes that its effects could be neutralized by some antidote, and this would be equivalent to saying that a cure had been found.

The mere fact, however, of finding D.M.P.E. in the urine of schizophrenics was not sufficient to establish that this substance was the cause of the disease. This new hypothesis had to be subjected to further tests; new facts had to be found which would either verify or falsify it. One obvious way of doing this was to give doses of D.M.P.E. to people not suffering from the disease; if the mere presence of the substance in the body was the cause, then the disease would be produced if it were introduced into the bodies of normal people. This was done, but no signs of schizophrenia resulted. The hypothesis, in the form expressed, had been falsified; but the presence of D.M.P.E. in the urine of people suffering from schizophrenia still remained a fact, and a new hypothesis had to be sought which would take this into account and, at the same time, explain why the presence of the chemical alone does not cause the disease.

66

This was done by Dr. Smythies, of Edinburgh University, who suggested that schizophrenics excrete D.M.P.E. because, through an inherited biochemical defect, they do not have the power to break it down within the body; the substance being harmless in those who do have this power. On this hypothesis, the presence of D.M.P.E. is merely an indication of a more fundamental biochemical disorder.

This still remains a hypothesis, and will not be accepted as a scientific truth until it has been rigorously tested. It may or may not explain the causes of schizophrenia, but in the meantime it opens up new areas for research; it tells scientists what kind of experiments are required—which is the main function of all hypotheses.

6. WHAT IS A SCIENCE?

Before a study is worthy of the name of science, it must make universal generalizations which enable us to explain some aspect of the world. Before we are justified in calling an explanation scientific, it must enable us to make predictions which can be tested by observation or experiment.

Acknowledged sciences vary considerably in their power to predict, and whether we think that a particular study should be called a science depends on the extent and accuracy of prediction we require before we think it worthy of that name. Meteorology, psychology, sociology, even history according to some historians, have claims to be considered scientific. They all have rigorous criteria for the collection of facts and they all, to some extent, attempt to formulate general laws; but, because of the complexity of their material, any predictions they make are far from reliable. The historian may see certain recurring patterns, but there are so many unknown factors in any historical situation that it is very doubtful whether any useful predictions can ever be made. The belief that history never repeats itself may be a surer guide to future conduct than any knowledge of past historical situations which may seem to resemble the one in which we find ourselves.

The power of prediction of mature sciences, such as physics, depends on the fact that all the relevant factors of a situation can be known and that anything which might falsify the result can be rigorously excluded. In subjects like meteorology, the number of facts which have to be known before a forecast can be made is so huge that complete accuracy is impossible.

Psychology, sociology and history, which study the behaviour of human beings, are always dealing with completely new individuals in completely new situations. Because no two people are ever exactly alike, and because they never have the same history, it is impossible to conclude that what has been true of one in the past will be true of the other in the future. Psychology often helps us to understand human behaviour, but the facts about people are so numerous and so difficult to discover that it is doubtful whether the psychologist will ever be able to make precise generalizations which will lead to accurate predictions. It may be true to say that John got angry because he was contradicted, but we cannot generalize from this and make the prediction that if John is contradicted tomorrow he will also get angry. There are many other factors which may intervene to prove us wrong. We may attribute someone's delinquency to a broken home, but we cannot make a general statement to the effect that whenever there is a broken home the children will become delinquent.

We may look upon human studies like psychology and sociology as scientific, but, for the most part, they are descriptive rather than predictive sciences. Like biology in the nineteenth century, they are more concerned with collecting facts than formulating general hypotheses or laws.

7. PSEUDO-SCIENCES

Hypotheses must enable predictions to be made, and these predictions have to be tested by comparison with what in fact happens. It is no use formulating a hypothesis which does not allow us to make any predictions and which consequently can never be shown to be true or false. The essential difference between a pseudo-science, such as astrology, and genuine sciences is that the former never runs the risk of being proved wrong by making a prediction. The astrologer's forecasts are so vague and unspecific that they can never be shown to be false.

The psychoanalytic theories of Freud, Adler and Jung claim to provide an explanation of human behaviour, but many of the things they put forward as scientific truths can never be subjected to any kind of test. For example, Adler says that pampering or lack of love and attention in childhood may, either of them, produce in the adult a neurotic feeling of inadequacy, an inability to cope with the real world, which he called an 'inferiority complex'. Now, according to this theory, an inferiority complex may manifest itself in various, and even opposite, ways. It sometimes makes people excessively shy and embarrassed and fearful of undertaking tasks in case they fail; it sometimes gives rise to behaviour which is boastful and aggressive, and may drive the person to undertake tasks which are far beyond his powers in order to show that, in reality, he is a superior kind of person.

Adler may well be right when he says that such behaviour has its origins in the person's early childhood, but the theory does not explain anything when it is compatible with such different results. It does not enable us to make any prediction about how a person will behave if he is treated in such and such a way in childhood, and thus it never exposes itself to the possibility of being proved wrong. Before it could be called a scientific theory, it would have to tell us how a person, with a certain kind of upbringing, would behave when he grew up. This it does not do.

If a hypothesis is put forward as an explanation of some aspect of the world as it is, its explanatory value depends on the possibility of its being proved false by the world being different from what the hypothesis had foretold. If the hypothesis still remains true whatever happens, then it is valueless as an explanation. A theory which claims to explain why things happen as they do, but which cannot conceivably be disproved, has no scientific basis.

FOR DISCUSSION AND ESSAYS

1. What do you understand by a science? Do you consider that mathematics, astronomy and psychology are sciences?
2. Discuss the part played by imagination in scientific discoveries.
3. Discuss the relative importance of deductive and inductive reasoning in scientific investigation.
4. 'Modern orthodox medicine belongs to the open-ended tradition of empirical science and sets up linked hypotheses which

are open to evidence both for and against. The intellectual regimes behind acupuncture, homeopathy, black boxes and so on are closed, a prioristic and intuitive.' (Jonathan Miller in *Observer*)

5. It has been said, 'Science does not prove anything; it disproves many things.' Discuss.

6. 'In observation, luck only favours minds prepared for it.' (Louis Pasteur)

7. 'If the principles of science needed only to be consistent, the world-systems of ingenious cranks would be true. Something more is needed for reliable knowledge in science, namely, experiment and observation, and conformity with them.'

8. 'The way of science is paved with discarded theories which were once declared self-evident.' (Karl Popper)
    What does this tell us about scientific method?

9. In *A Liberal Education*, T. H. Huxley wrote: 'The mental power which will be of most importance in your life will be the power of seeing things as they are without regard to authority.' Show how this lies at the basis of all scientific progress.

10. 'In our search for truth, we have replaced scientific certainty by scientific progress.' (Karl Popper)

11. 'Scientific progress, considered historically, is not a strictly logical process, and does not proceed by syllogisms.' (Larmor)

12. 'A theory which is not refutable by any conceivable event is non-scientific.' (Karl Popper)

13. 'How odd it is that anyone should not see that all observation must be for or against some view if it is to be of any service.' (Charles Darwin)

14. 'Induction is a habit of the human mind which cannot be justified by any purely formal methods but which it is none the less unreasonable not to adopt.' (F. P. Ramsey)

15. 'The discovery of instances which confirm a theory means very little if we have not tried, and failed, to discover refutations.' (Karl Popper)

CHAPTER 4

ETHICS

I. MORAL LANGUAGE

(a) *Analytic and Empirical Statements*

When we have a closed system of thinking, like logic and mathematics, the truth or falsity of the statements we make depends, as it were, on our following the rules of the game. Unless we make some error of calculation or reasoning, we can be certain of the correctness of our conclusions. We know that the statement 'All husbands are males' is true, for the obvious reason that we apply the word 'husband' only to males. We do not need to be acquainted with any husbands; we only need to know what the word means. We can be said to know that this analytic statement is true, prior to any experience, and so knowledge of this kind is called *a priori* knowledge.

When we have an open system of thinking, when, that is, we are talking about the world around us, we no longer have this built-in guarantee of the truth of our statements. When we make specific statements about our environment, such as 'The water is cold', or when we make generalizations like 'Water expands on freezing', their truth depends on evidence which we obtain through our senses. We cannot know *a priori* that the water is cold; it is an empirical observation. Nor can we tell that water expands on freezing by analysing the meaning of the word 'water'; it is not an analytic, but an empirical truth.

Whenever we are in doubt about the truth of a statement, it is first of all necessary to ask ourselves how we ought to set about verifying it; that is, whether it is analytic or empirical. We need to know whether the truth of the statement depends on a correct analysis of the meaning of words, or on supporting empirical evidence. It is not until we are clear on this point that we can hope to be in a position to accept or reject the statement as true.

We soon discover, however, that there are certain statements which do not seem to fit into either of these two categories. If someone says 'Cruelty is wrong', we should all agree that it is true, but if someone were to deny it, how should we set about proving him mistaken? It is not an analytic statement, for there is nothing in the meaning of the word 'cruelty' which necessitates its being wrong. On the other hand, if it is empirical, through which of the senses do we receive information which is evidence for its truth? It does not seem to be analytic or empirical, and if there is no way of verifying it, does it make sense to say that it is true or false?

It is not difficult to think of a large number of statements of this kind which we frequently make, where it is not at all clear how we can know whether they are true or false. 'Shakespeare is the world's greatest dramatist', 'Paris is a beautiful city', 'Asparagus is better than cabbage', 'Cricket is a boring game', 'Pleasure is the only good', 'It is your duty to help the weak' are all statements of this kind. It is possible to deny them all without breaking any rules of logic and without refusing to accept the evidence of the senses.

If someone prefers asparagus to cabbage, or thinks that cricket is a boring game, we conclude that it is all a matter of taste. We should be less inclined to think it merely a matter of taste if someone thought Shakespeare was not the world's greatest dramatist, still less so if he were to maintain that it is not our duty to help the weak.

We are much more ready to tolerate differences of belief in literary or artistic matters than in morality. No serious consequences are likely to flow from people believing that boogie-woogie is better than Beethoven, but if they believe that the white races of the world are inherently superior to the coloured races, the result could be disastrous. It is because our moral beliefs affect our conduct that they assume such importance. Morality is primarily concerned with our relationship with other people, and it is the things we consider right and wrong and our conception of what we ought or ought not to do that determine our attitudes and actions towards our fellows. None of us can, therefore, be indifferent to the moral beliefs of others, for the simple reason that we cannot escape the actions which follow from these beliefs.

(b) Ethics and Morality

There are two different ways of approaching any study of morality. On the one hand, we can think of it as an organized system of rules of conduct which tell us what we should do and what we should avoid doing. From such a study we should learn that it is wrong to tell lies and right to relieve suffering; it would provide us with the kind of advice we expect from our parents or our elders or the church about how we should behave. The parent or parson who says 'It is wrong to tell lies' is indulging in a form of moral propaganda and hopes that he will, in this way, influence conduct. The study of the content of moral statements, offering guidance about what actions are right or wrong, we shall call 'Morality'.

On the other hand, we can approach moral questions by studying the different moral beliefs in the way we have already done with analytic and empirical statements. That is, we can examine moral statements in order to discover precisely what they mean and how we can decide whether they are true or false. When someone says that it is wrong to tell lies, we can ask him what he means by the word 'wrong', and on what grounds it can be applied to lying. The branch of philosophy which analyses the meaning of moral words, such as 'duty', 'good' and 'bad', 'right' and 'wrong', we shall call 'Ethics'.

Thus the student of morality asks the question 'What is good?', to which the answer might be 'Pleasure is good' or 'Health is good'; he wants to know what things are good. The student of ethics asks 'What is "good"?' and this is a question about the word 'good', and not about things. It is only after the moralist has decided upon his answers that the ethical philosopher begins to ask his questions. When the moralist says 'Pleasure is good' or 'It is wrong to tell lies', the ethical philosopher is not concerned to dispute these statements, but to wonder what is meant by the words 'good' and 'wrong'.

Only when we are clear in our minds about the meaning these words are given in a statement can we profitably discuss whether the statement is true or false. Before two people can have a profitable discussion about whether abortion, or homosexuality, is right or wrong, they must clarify what they mean by these moral terms.

(c) Moral and Non-Moral Use of 'Good'

If someone were to ask you what exactly you mean by 'good' when you say that happiness is good, or by 'right' when you say that it is right to tell the truth, what answer would you give? The words 'good' and 'right' are adjectives, but they do not seem to function like other adjectives. 'Round' and 'square' refer to particular qualities in an object, but is there anything we can point to, or isolate, which corresponds to 'good'? When we call an action 'deliberate' or 'hurried', we are referring to particular observable characteristics, but what are we referring to when we call it 'right'? Although we know how to use 'good' and 'bad', 'right' and 'wrong', it is extremely difficult to analyse precisely what they mean.

In the first place, we can use them in either a moral or a non-moral sense. If we say of someone that he is a good cricketer but a bad man, we are using 'good' in a non-moral, and 'bad' in a moral sense. It is quite wrong for the wicket-keeper to take the ball in front of the wicket if he wants to stump the batsman, but it is not morally wrong. It is morally wrong to be cruel to children or to tell lies.

In their non-moral use, these words have something in common with ordinary adjectives. If we say 'This is a good table', we are referring primarily to certain empirical qualities which the table has, such as its firmness, the smoothness of its polished surface and the convenience of its drawers. Different people may have different ideas of what particular qualities are necessary before they are prepared to call a table good, but they would all have in mind a number of things which can be specifically referred to and observed. Unlike 'round', 'black' or 'smooth', 'good' seems to be an omnibus word which is used to refer to several distinct properties at once. But, because we apply 'good' to many things which are strikingly different from one another, there is no limit to the number of qualities which can be indicated by its use.

Motor cars and penknives, priests and footballers, beer and bread can all be good, but there is no common property which they all possess. One of the qualities which makes a penknife good is the sharpness of its blades, but this quality is not to be found in motor cars. A footballer is good because he is skilful in the use of his feet, but this would hardly seem to be what makes a priest good. The word does not stand for any one empirical quality which we can point to in the object: things which are good seem to be so for different reasons.

74

(d) *Analysis of Ethical Words*

It is even less clear what qualities are referred to when such words as 'good' and 'bad', 'right' and 'wrong' are used in the purely moral sense. When we talk of actions as being gentle, or violent, we are referring to qualities which can be seen to belong to the actions themselves; 'gentle' and 'violent' are quite obviously descriptive words. When, however, we talk of actions as being right or wrong, we are immediately puzzled as to what specific qualities these words stand for. There does not seem to be any quality, or property, which we can point to in an action which makes it right or wrong.

When we discussed the non-moral use of the word 'good', for example when we talked of a 'good penknife', we found that we were able to point to particular characteristics, such as sharpness and design, which, when added together, make a penknife 'good'. We may not all agree about what these qualities are, because we may use penknives for different purposes, but for each one of us, 'good' would refer to a particular set of characteristics which we expect a good penknife to have. Although we may apply the word differently, we have a fairly clear idea of what it means, and differences which arise about whether something is good or bad may be resolved when we make explicit the particular properties we have in mind when we use these words. In addition to the purely descriptive meaning, however, there is the sense that we approve of or attach value to whatever is described. A good motor car is one which we think well of because it has certain qualities, but the word 'good' also says something about the way we feel about it; that is, it has an evaluative as well as a descriptive meaning.

If two people disagree about whether a radio set is good or bad, it is probably because they are looking for different things; it may be that for one of them a good set must have, above all, quality reproduction, whereas for the other it must be good to look at. They may agree that the set has very good reproduction, which is why one of them thought it good, and also that it is not very good to look at, which is why the other thought it bad. By stating, in purely natural and descriptive terms, the meaning each one attaches to the word 'good', they are able to see more precisely what it is they are disagreeing about, but each one will continue

75

to attach the same value to the particular quality which the word describes. They have explained why they think a certain kind of radio good or bad, but this will not, in itself, change their evaluative judgement of radios.

When we come to the moral use of the word 'good', we find that we are not able to break it down in this way; there are no natural properties we can point to which add up to its moral meaning.

If moral terms can be given non-moral meanings, if we can find equivalents which refer to observable, natural qualities, this will enable us to see more clearly what moral disagreements are about. Some philosophers have believed that they could do this, and thus turn moral statements into empirical ones. If natural equivalents can be found for 'good' and 'wrong' in 'Pleasure is good' and 'It is wrong to tell lies', then we can decide whether these statements are true or false by observing whether these natural qualities are present or absent. The various attempts which have been made to give moral terms non-moral, natural meanings are called Naturalistic Theories.

There are two kinds of Naturalistic Theory according to whether the natural properties described are thought of as being objective or subjective. We talk of things in our environment, such as trees and motor cars, as 'objective', and contrast them with mental occurrences, such as dreams and emotions, which we call 'subjective'. Objective Naturalistic Theories claim that, just as the adjectives 'round' or 'square', 'hard' or 'soft' refer objectively to qualities which exist in the things described, so 'good' and 'bad', 'right' and 'wrong' refer to objective, natural qualities of things or actions. Subjective Naturalistic Theories say that moral words do not refer to qualities which exist outside the observer, but describe subjective experiences. If I say 'Your father is very angry' or 'I feel rather tired', the adjectives 'angry' and 'tired' refer to states of mind and not to external objects; 'good' and 'bad', it is claimed, perform a similar function.

2. NATURALISTIC THEORIES

(a) Objective

The most widely known attempt to explain moral words in terms of an objective, natural quality was made by two British philosophers of the nineteenth century, Jeremy Bentham and John Stuart Mill. They put forward the theory that when we say an action is right, all we mean is that it produces a greater amount of happiness than any other action could have in the circumstances. This is an ethical, not a moral, theory, because it is about the meaning of the word 'right' and not about what kind of actions are right. Bentham and Mill also put forward a moral theory, which says that right actions are those which produce the greatest amount of happiness, but this must not be confused with the ethical theory, which is concerned only with the meaning of the moral term used.

The moral theory sets out to answer the question 'What is right?', and answers it by giving the criterion by which we can judge rightness. The ethical theory asks the question 'What is "right"?', and answers by saying that 'right' means 'productive of happiness'. Both these theories are given the name 'Utilitarianism', but it is the moral form of the theory, the one which enables us to judge which actions are right, that has had the greatest influence and is generally thought of when Utilitarianism is mentioned.

We shall have more to say later about Utilitarianism as a moral theory, but in this chapter we are discussing it as an ethical theory, that is, as a theory about what ethical words mean.

According to Bentham and Mill, when we say 'It is right to tell the truth', what we mean is 'Telling the truth produces the greatest amount of happiness'. Now, although it is not easy to measure happiness, or to compare the amounts produced by different actions, happiness is something we all understand, and, if 'right' means 'productive of happiness', we have discovered a way of turning moral into empirical statements. Thus, 'You did right to refuse his request' would be equivalent to 'By refusing his request you have increased the sum of happiness' and this, in theory at least, could be tested empirically.

Bentham and Mill both believed that if they could, in this way, reduce the meaning of moral terms to something which could be expressed in objective, natural terms, then they could build up a science of morals. Mill, particularly, was much impressed by the growth of scientific knowledge in the nineteenth century, and wanted to find a means of including moral statements in the total of human knowledge. He understood how analytic and empirical statements could be verified and how new knowledge was obtained by deduction and induction. If there was to be moral knowledge, it was necessary to show that moral statements were, in reality, a special kind of empirical statement, and this could only be done by finding non-moral, or natural, equivalents for moral words.

There is, however, a fatal objection to any such attempt. If 'right' really did mean 'productive of happiness', it would not be possible both to agree that an action was productive of happiness and wonder whether it was right. But this is something which we frequently do. A schoolmaster may agree that excusing a form homework will make them happy, but still wonder whether it is the right thing to do. This would be impossible if 'right' meant 'productive of happiness'.

We can understand this fallacy more clearly if we look at it in conjunction with Utilitarianism as a moral theory. As a moral theory, Utilitarianism says that the right and proper end of human action is the greatest happiness of the greatest number; as an ethical theory, it says that 'right' means 'productive of happiness'. If we put these two theories together, we get the result that the moral theory 'An action which produces the greatest amount of happiness is right' means 'An action which produces the greatest amount of happiness produces the greatest amount of happiness'. This absurdity arises from the attempt of Bentham and Mill to define moral words in terms of natural qualities; whatever natural equivalents we substitute for moral words, we shall be faced with the same absurdity. There is always some part of the moral meaning left over which the natural equivalent does not cover. It is this extra meaning of moral words which explains why we can agree that an action possesses the natural quality which is thought to be the equivalent of the moral word, and still wonder whether it is right. To believe that there are such natural equivalents is to commit what G. E. Moore called the 'Naturalistic Fallacy'.

(b) Subjective

According to the Subjectivist, when we say 'Cruelty is always wrong', the moral term 'wrong' does not refer to an objective quality in the act, but to a subjective feeling, or attitude, we have towards it. All moral terms are, he believes, descriptive of natural characteristics, but they are subjective, not objective, ones. When we say that things are good or bad, right or wrong, we are not talking about the things as such, but about our feelings towards them.

Now, feelings are natural phenomena, and any statements about them are empirical, not moral. It follows, therefore, that if the person who says 'Cruelty is always wrong' is truthfully reporting his feelings, then the statement is true; but if he does not have these feelings, then the statement is false. All that a person need do in order to verify or falsify a moral statement is to make sure that he is correctly reporting his feelings or attitude. But it also means that what looked like a moral statement about human conduct turns out to be an empirical statement about the contents of a person's mind.

What gives a certain plausibility to this theory is the fact that people often have different ideas about what is good and bad, right and wrong. According to the Subjectivist, this difference can best be accounted for if we try to understand the meaning of moral terms, not by comparing them to straightforward descriptive adjectives like red, round, smooth and hard, but to adjectives like exciting, interesting and pleasing, which do not describe objective properties, but subjective feelings. If I say 'This book is red', I am obviously referring to something which can be verified by the sense of sight, but if I say 'This book is interesting' I am talking primarily about the way I feel towards it. Perhaps the same approach will prove fruitful for ethical terms. If someone says 'Happiness is good' or 'Telling the truth is right', maybe he is talking of nothing but his own feelings.

This certainly seems to be the case when two people disagree about matters of taste. For example, I may see a painting of Picasso's and say 'That is a good painting', and if I am asked to give reasons why I think it is good, I may refer to its use of colour or its form or some other characteristic. But if I am pressed by a companion, who knows as much about painting as I do, and who suggests reasons why he thinks it is not a good painting, I may be reduced to saying 'Well, in spite of what you say, I still like it'. In fact, I may be quite prepared to admit that when I say 'It is a good painting', I am really saying 'I like the painting'.

I am not suggesting that in matters of art this is always the case;

it is quite possible to realize that a certain work of art is good without liking it. Nevertheless, for many people, it would be true to say that 'I think X is good' is equivalent to 'I like X'.

Can we say the same thing when 'good' is used in a moral sense? When I say 'Honesty is a good quality', am I merely saying 'I like honesty'? And when I say 'It is right to tell the truth', do I mean any more than 'I like people to tell the truth'?

A few moments' thought will show us that there are many actions which we may like but which we should hesitate to call right. We may like to stay in bed in the mornings, but we do not necessarily think it is the right thing to do. If all we mean when we say that an action is right is that we like doing it, then there can never be any sense in saying that we like doing right actions, for this would be equivalent to saying that we like doing the actions we like doing.

But if we cannot say that 'X is right' is equivalent to 'I like X', maybe there is another verb which expresses more accurately the feeling we have when we say that an action is right. Would it be more correct to say that 'X is right' means 'I approve of X'? It is true that we usually disapprove of actions which we think wrong, even though we may like doing them; approving and disapproving have a moral flavour which is lacking in liking and disliking.

If, when I say 'X is right', all I mean is that I approve of X, and when you say 'X is right', all you mean is that you approve of X, then 'right' means something different for each of us. On the same assumption, when I say that X is right and you say that X is wrong, we are not disagreeing, because we are talking about different things. I am saying that X arouses feelings of approval in me, and you are saying that X raises feelings of disapproval in you, and both these statements may be true. In fact X may be both right and wrong at the same time.

If this is the true meaning of 'right', then there can never be moral arguments. It would mean that when A says 'Fox hunting is wrong' and B says 'Fox hunting is right', they would not be disagreeing, because they would be talking about different things. A would be talking about the feelings that fox hunting arouses in him, whereas B would be talking about his own feelings and not those of A. Unless we are prepared to accept that there can never be any disagreements on moral questions, we must reject the theory that the ethical terms 'good' and 'right' mean that the person who uses them approves of whatever they qualify.

(c) Some Dangers of Subjectivism

The belief that moral terms derive their meaning from the feelings or attitudes of certain individuals or sections of society is often used to justify pressure on minorities who hold moral principles not acceptable to the majority. If all we mean when we say that it is wrong to tell lies is that lying is disapproved of by most members of society, then all pressures towards conformity are morally justified. All we should need to do to discover whether something is good, or an action is right, would be to take a referendum or consult an opinion poll. Is capital punishment morally defensible? If 51 per cent of the population say it is right to hang murderers, then hanging is right. It would be absurd to maintain that hanging is wrong and at the same time believe that the meaning of 'wrong' is 'disapproved of by most people'.

This theory would mean that it would be immoral of minorities to try to make majorities change their moral outlook, for the simple reason that, being minorities, they would be trying to make people do actions which are wrong.

It is sometimes suggested that 'right' means 'approved by God'. Like the other naturalistic theories we have discussed, this is an attempt to reduce the ethical to the factual, or empirical. 'This action is right' is a moral statement, whereas 'This action is approved by God' is empirical. If this were the true meaning of 'right', people who do not believe in God could not make moral judgements, but they quite clearly do so, even if they are misguided ones.

We must also be clear about whether we are saying that 'right' *means* 'approved by God' or that God approves what is right. It is one thing to say that God never approves anything which is wrong, and quite another to say that, when we talk of an action being wrong, we mean that God disapproves it. I think that what most religious people believe is that God never approves anything which is wrong; that is, that ethical terms have a meaning of their own, irrespective of whether God approves them or not. If 'good' and 'right' have no meaning apart from God's approval or disapproval, it would be impossible to talk of God approving what was right, for 'God approves what is right' would mean 'God approves what God approves'.

3. OUGHT AND IS

All the theories we have been considering are attempts to do the same thing: to find natural or descriptive equivalents for ethical terms. If we could equate ethical statements with empirical statements or with psychological or sociological facts about some people or most people, then we should have achieved Mill's ambition of a science of ethics. How often we hear the remark that man's moral development has not kept pace with his scientific and technical progress! If we could turn ethics into a science, we should be able to demonstrate the truth of moral statements and improve our moral understanding as we acquired more factual knowledge.

A scientist can start from a generalization about nature, such as 'Water expands on freezing', and from the fact that the water in a particular pipe freezes he can deduce that this water expands. We can arrange this deduction in the form of a syllogism, and say:

> Water expands on freezing.
> This water is freezing.
> Therefore this water is expanding.

Now, the moral philosopher does not find himself in such a fortunate position. Such straightforward pieces of deductive reasoning, which give conclusions everyone is prepared to accept, are not to be found in ethics. The first person to draw attention to this fact was David Hume, and what he had to say has had a profound effect on all subsequent thinking on the subject. The relevant passage is of such importance in the study of ethics, and has become so well known, that I will quote it in full.

'I cannot forbear adding to these reasonings an observation which may perhaps be found of some importance. In every system of morality which I have hitherto met with I have always remarked that the author proceeds for some time in the ordinary way of reasoning, and establishes the being of a God, or makes observations concerning human affairs; when of a sudden I am surprised to find, that instead of the usual copulations of propositions, *is* and *is not*, I meet with no proposition that is not connected with an *ought* or an *ought not*. This change is imperceptible; but is, however, of the last consequence. For as this *ought* or *ought not* expresses some new relation or affirmation, it is necessary that it should be observed and explained; and at the same time that a reason should be given for what seems altogether inconceivable, how this new relation can be a deduction from others that are entirely different from it.'

Hume is criticizing those philosophers who start with certain facts about the universe, which are expressed in statements containing the words *is* or *is not*, and then deduce from these statements others which do not contain *is* or *is not*, but *ought* or *ought not*. Now, in a deductive argument, it is not possible that there should be something in the conclusion which is not included in the premises. If there is no *ought* or *ought not* in one of the premises, it cannot validly be deduced in the conclusion. From statements of fact about what is or is not the case, we cannot logically deduce that anything ought or ought not to be done; we cannot derive an *ought* from an *is*. Failure to understand this lies at the root of much muddled thinking in ethical matters.

This can be illustrated by an example. When we say 'The atom bomb killed thousands of people in Hiroshima', we are making a statement of fact. It is the kind of statement we are prepared to accept as true because we know how it can be verified. If, however, we say 'They ought not to have dropped the bomb on Hiroshima', we are not making a statement of fact, and it is not at all clear how we should set about verifying it. From the statement that thousands of people were killed at Hiroshima, we cannot logically deduce anything about what ought or ought not to have been done. We may feel that because thousands of people were killed the bomb ought not to have been dropped, but another person cannot logically be refuted if he maintains that the bomb ought to have been dropped.

There are arguments we can use to try to make him change his mind. We might point to the great suffering of the victims, or to the probable harmful effects on unborn generations, but we should only be adding further facts of the same kind and, as we have seen, no conclusion about what ought to be done can be deduced from a mere piling up of facts about what has been done. This does not mean that the accumulation of facts does not have any effect, in practice, on a person's moral attitudes. We are not indeed justified in adopting a moral attitude to any question without a full knowledge of the facts, and the manner of their presentation is often of great importance in determining moral attitudes. But this is not the point at issue. What I am trying to make clear is that there is no *logical* reason why one moral conclusion rather than another should follow from simple statements of fact.

Before we can arrive at a conclusion which tells us what we ought to do, we must have an 'ought' in one of the premises. Thus, if we can agree on the premise 'We ought not to cause suffering', we can rewrite our argument as follows:

> We ought not to cause suffering.
> Dropping the bomb on Hiroshima caused great suffering.
> Therefore we ought not to have dropped the bomb on Hiroshima.

This is now a perfectly valid argument, because we are deducing a moral conclusion from a moral premise, and not trying to do so from premises which are purely factual.

In moral discussions of all kinds, attempts are often made to blur the distinction between the moral and the factual, and thus conceal the invalidity of an argument. For example, someone may try to show that it is wrong to use contraceptives by arguing as follows:

> Marriage exists for the procreation of children.
> Contraceptives prevent procreation.
> Therefore contraceptives should not be used.

If the first premise is a statement of fact, that when people marry they always do so in order to have children, then it does not allow us to deduce from it any conclusion about what people ought to do. If, on the other hand, it is a concealed moral judgement about what marriage ought to be for, then the argument is valid but begs the whole question. Once we concede the premise, of course we accept the conclusion, but the whole argument is about whether we should concede the premise. It is by making a moral judgement look like a statement of fact, that it is hoped to get the conclusion accepted.

Sociologists, economists, psychologists and others often try to persuade us that moral conclusions can be derived from factual statements about the human mind or social behaviour. People have sometimes argued that because man is by nature a warlike animal, we should not consider it morally wrong to fight wars. Because of human nature it may be very difficult to abolish all wars, but we cannot deduce any moral principle from this fact. It is important always to be fully alive to this distinction between the factual and the moral.

The statement 'All men are equal' is often thought to justify the claim that people should be treated in the same way and given the same opportunities in life. This is a very laudable moral ideal, but it does not logically follow from the empirical statement, even if it were true, that all men are equal. It is another example of a moral judgement masquerading as a statement of fact. When people say 'All men are equal', they do not really mean that they are, in fact, equal, but that they ought to be treated as such.

It is sometimes said that there can be no morality without a religious basis. This could mean two different things. On the one hand, it might be an empirical statement to the effect that people without religious beliefs lead immoral lives. This could be verified or falsified by a social survey. It might not be easy to decide what constitutes religious belief, or to agree precisely on what lives are immoral; nevertheless, some empirical enquiry would be necessary before we could know whether the claim was justified. If we found that all the inhabitants of our prisons had no religious beliefs, this might be considered to be supporting evidence. If we found that the proportion of believers inside the prisons was the same as outside, we might be inclined to believe that the claim had no basis in fact.

On the other hand, it might mean that no one is justified in holding moral beliefs unsupported by religious ones. Such a claim, however, cannot stand, because ethical judgements cannot be logically deduced from religious statements, any more than they can from psychological or sociological ones. We cannot deduce the moral conclusion that we ought to do a particular action from the statement that it is commanded by God, unless we are already committed to the moral imperative that we ought to do what God commands. The following is a valid deductive argument:

I ought to do what God commands.
God commands that I should be truthful.
Therefore I ought to be truthful.

85

It would not, however, be valid without the moral premise.

A religious faith is made up of belief in the truth of certain empirical statements and also the acceptance of certain moral commands. When we have a religious faith, as well as believing that certain events happened, we accept that there are some things we ought or ought not to do, that some actions are right and others wrong. That is, we have already made certain moral commitments; we have not deduced, nor can we deduce, these from the religious statements of fact which we believe to be true.

Thus, a system of morality does not logically need a religious basis.

4. NON-NATURALISTIC THEORIES

(a) Intuitionism

(i) Descriptive or Evaluative?

Naturalistic theories say that it is possible to explain the meaning of ethical terms by means of other terms which are purely descriptive, or natural. Most modern philosophers are of the opinion that this is not possible because, whatever natural property we think 'good' or 'right' refers to, it is always possible to agree that the property is present and still ask whether the thing is good. For example, if 'good' means 'pleasant', it would be logically impossible to agree that something is pleasant and at the same time to wonder whether it is good, but in practice we often do make such a distinction. I may find it pleasant to drink a lot of whisky and yet wonder whether it is good for me to do so. If 'good' meant 'pleasant', such a thought would be impossible.

G. E. Moore, having pointed out the fallacy in all such naturalistic explanations, went on to argue that ethical terms do refer to characteristics or properties, but that they are not natural ones. We are aware, according to Moore, of ethical properties in things or actions, just as we are aware of natural properties, but not through the ordinary senses. We do not see, hear or feel these non-natural properties, we *intuit* them in some way; hence the name Intuitionism for all theories of this kind.

But, Moore believed, if we try to explain to someone the meaning of 'good', we are attempting an impossible task. Can we explain to a blind man the meaning of yellow? A colour is something we experience but cannot define. In the words of G. E. Moore, from his *Principia Ethica*, '... as you cannot, by any manner of means, explain to anyone who does not already know it, what yellow is, so you cannot explain what good is'.

When we say that happiness is good, we cannot express what we mean in any other way, but we feel sure that happiness does possess this indefinable quality. In the same way, we feel instinctively that some actions possess the property of being right and others of being wrong. In the view of the Intuitionist, it is self-evident that it is right to be kind and truthful.

The great attraction of this view is that it seems to avoid the naturalistic fallacy. The Naturalist tries to establish the truth of ethical statements by finding natural equivalents for moral words: the Intuitionist, by insisting that we can be directly aware of ethical properties in things or actions, hopes to abolish the gap between the empirical and the ethical.

When the Naturalist defines 'right' as 'conducive to happiness', it is possible to agree that an action is conducive to happiness and still ask whether it is right, or why one ought to do it. But if the rightness of an action is a moral property which we intuit, is this not equivalent to saying that the action ought to be done? The property being a moral one, is it logically possible to agree that the action has this property and still wonder whether it ought to be done? 'It is right to tell the truth' means, for the Intuitionist, that telling the truth possesses a special property which we can intuit, and which we call 'right'. This property is of such a kind that we cannot be aware of its presence and still wonder whether we ought to tell the truth. The obligation is built into the meaning of the word, and we cannot accept the word and refuse the obligation.

The Intuitionist, by saying that the rightness of an action is a moral property, is trying to ensure that ethical judgements remain empirical statements and at the same time retain their moral force. The Naturalist failed because there is no logical connection between a statement that an action A possesses a certain property and a moral judgement that one ought to do A. The Intuitionist tries to get round this difficulty by saying that ethical words describe ethical properties, but in such a way that they prescribe what ought to be done.

87

Now, if something is good, it is because it has certain natural characteristics or properties; this is true whether the word is used in the non-moral or moral sense. In so far as 'good' refers to these natural characteristics, it is used descriptively, but this descriptive part of the meaning does not exhaust all we mean when we use the word. If we use 'good' in the non-moral sense, in addition to the descriptive meaning, we are indicating that we value the object described. As we saw earlier, when we call a motor car good, it is because it has particular empirical properties—safety, reliability, comfort—but, in addition, we are stating that we value these properties. That is, 'good' has both a descriptive and an evaluative meaning.

When we use 'good' in a moral sense as, for example, when we speak of someone's 'good deed', we are both describing the deed and also saying that we approve of it and recommend it to others. The word 'good' is being used in two ways, descriptively and evaluatively, but these two meanings still remain distinct; we cannot say that 'good' is purely descriptive, and then use it evaluatively to deduce a moral conclusion. We cannot bridge the logical gap between the descriptive and the evaluative by saying that, because 'good' has both meanings, the gap does not exist.

The Intuitionist says that the ethical word 'right' describes a property and also establishes an obligation, but in so far as 'right' is descriptive it refers to a property, and in so far as it is evaluative it refers to an attitude. The gap between the empirical and the ethical is still there. Whether we define 'good' and 'right' in naturalistic or non-naturalistic terms, in so far as these words are descriptive of a property, they cannot carry an evaluative meaning. From the fact that such and such is the case, I cannot logically deduce that I ought to do such and such.

(ii) Differences of Intuition

There is another difficulty with the theory of Intuitionism, namely, how to recognize the unique ethical property which the Intuitionist claims to intuit. When we refer to natural, empirical properties, we usually have a fairly clear idea of what we are looking for and how to recognize them when they are present. But what are we to say about these supposed non-natural properties—odd, mysterious and elusive things?

Intuitionists claim that we have an inner moral sense which functions in a manner analogous to our sense of sight; we 'see' moral properties with a kind of 'inner eye'. Just as we can use the sense of sight and say 'This book is red', so we can use this special moral faculty, or inner sight, to say 'That action you did yesterday was wrong'. Both statements, they believe, can be true or false, because they are attributing properties to things which may or may not have them. But are we satisfied that these two statements are really alike? Disagreements about the colour of a book can usually be resolved; we may differ about what name we shall give to a particular shade of red, whether to call it crimson or scarlet, but we are hardly ever in doubt about the presence of the property, red. Someone who is colour blind may demur for a while, but in the end he will give way and the truth will be established. But what about the rightness of an action? If A's moral sense tells him that an action is right, but B's tells him that it is wrong, how would they set about resolving their disagreement? With empirical statements based on sense experience, we know how they can be verified or falsified, but how can we decide between different intuitions?

The Intuitionist sets out to give us ethical judgements which can be true or false, but completely fails to supply any way of deciding between truth or falsehood. It is not much help to provide a theory which tells us that 'Truthfulness is right' is a statement which can be true or false, if he is unable to supply us with some means of deciding which it is. When two people disagree about whether an action is right, a theory that rightness is a property does not help them to decide which of them is in possession of the truth, unless the presence of the property can be clearly and convincingly demonstrated. And this is what Intuitionism fails to do.

When A says that an action X possesses the property P, which makes it right, and B says that it does not, does it not seem more plausible to suggest that A and B are expressing their own attitudes to the action, rather than talking about a mysterious moral property?

If objective moral properties really do exist, moral disagreement would seem to indicate that there is a perverse refusal, on the part of one side, to take sufficient care with his intuition. In disagreements over empirical matters we do not, as a rule, encounter this difficulty; factual disagreements about what we see and hear can usually be settled. If, therefore, there are moral properties, just as there are empirical ones, and people still persist in their moral disagreements, it must be the result, not of genuine differences about what they intuit, but of deliberate obtuseness. The belief that moral disagreements can be explained in this way leads inevitably to intolerance. If we believe that ethical judgements are essentially expressions of attitudes, then moral disagreements seem natural and acceptable, but if they are descriptive of certain features of the external world, then these disagreements are surprising, and there is a temptation to think that they should be eradicated. It is no coincidence that some of the most intolerant doctrines throughout history have been based on intuitive theories of ethics. That these theories have often had this unfortunate result is, of course, quite irrelevant to their truth; if we reject them it must be on other grounds.

These theories may owe their origin to the fallacy that we can elucidate the meanings of words by discovering what it is they refer to. We have, however, already seen that, because a word has connotation, it does not follow that it must also have denotation. When we ask for the meaning of 'good' and 'right', it is important to remember that it is essentially the person who uses the words who means something, and not the words themselves. This does not mean that words do not sometimes refer to external properties, but that they do not always so refer. Because such adjectives as 'round', 'square', 'soft' and 'hard' do refer to properties, we must not assume that moral adjectives such as 'good' and 'bad', 'right' and 'wrong' also refer to them. Adjectives are used in different ways and perform different functions, as we shall see in the next section.

(b) Emotivism

(i) Expression and Description

The Subjective Naturalist says that moral words describe attitudes or feelings, the Intuitionist that they describe objective non-natural properties, the Emotivist claims that they do not *describe*, but *express* emotions or attitudes.

When a father says to his son 'It is wrong to beat your sister', he is, according to the Subjective Naturalist, describing the way he feels about his son's beating his sister. If he really does feel this way, then what he is saying is true, but if he does not, the statement is false. According to the Intuitionist, the parent observes an objective property in the action of beating; just as he can see that it is violent, so he can, in some analogous fashion, 'see' that it is wrong.

The Emotivist believes that the father is not *describing* anything, but is *expressing* his own feeling of disapproval. This Emotive Theory of Ethics, or Emotivism, is based on the fact that not all adjectives are used to refer to properties, and that the specifically moral meaning of ethical terms is not descriptive at all.

We must be careful to distinguish this theory from the subjective naturalistic theory, which says that the meaning of 'X is good' is 'I approve of X'. The Subjective Naturalist holds that an ethical statement can be reduced to a factual one, and that when someone says 'This action is wrong', all he means is 'I disapprove of this action'. The Emotivist says that the statement 'This action is wrong' is not really a statement at all, but an expression of the speaker's attitude to the action.

Both the Subjective Naturalist and the Emotivist realize that morality is fundamentally based on feelings or attitudes; where the Subjective Naturalist is mistaken is in thinking that moral utterances are statements *about* our feelings or attitudes. Because we say 'Cruelty is wrong' as a result of certain feelings we have, it must not be assumed that what we are talking about is our feelings. The statement may be causally explicable in terms of human emotions, but it is not a statement *about* human emotions. There is a fundamental difference between making a statement about an emotion and expressing an emotion.

The Subjective Naturalist and the Intuitionist both believe that moral statements are empirical; for the former they describe subjective feelings, whereas for the latter they refer to non-natural properties. For the Emotivist, they are not statements at all, but value judgements, which express a person's feelings or attitude; to say 'Murder is wrong' is not to say something which can be true or false, but to express an emotion, as if to say 'Murder—Shame!'.

(ii) *Emotive Meaning of Words*

We have already referred to the way ordinary adjectives can have both a descriptive and an emotive meaning. To call a man firm is to describe certain of his qualities, and, in addition, to make the hearer understand that these qualities are admired. To call a man obstinate may be to attribute to him the same qualities as those possessed by the firm man, but it is not to express admiration for them. 'Firm' and 'obstinate' have both a descriptive and an emotive content.

Many moral words seem to have both a descriptive and an emotive element. If we call someone trustworthy, we are partly describing the kind of person he is, and partly expressing our approval of him. 'He is a good father' would be indicative of the speaker's approval today, as well as in Victorian Britain, but the descriptive meaning of the words would not be the same. A Victorian's idea of a good father would involve qualities of sternness and aloofness which would hardly find favour today, but the degree of approval for the two different conceptions would be the same.

The Intuitionist and the Emotivist base their theories on the assumption that moral words must be either descriptive or emotive, whereas there seem to be good reasons for holding that they can be both. As far as ethics is concerned, however, it is the emotive element of the meaning which is important. Moral words are primarily concerned, not with describing behaviour, but with the more practical question of directing it. The description of the way people behave is the province of the psychologist, or the sociologist, or the anthropologist; the moral philosopher is concerned with how they ought to behave. We do not make moral judgements in order to describe what people do, nor do we make them as mere expressions of our own attitudes. Their most important function is to influence behaviour and to persuade others to do what we think is right.

In order to influence behaviour, in order to persuade people to follow certain moral principles, moral judgements must do more than express the attitude of the person who utters them. 'It is wrong to drink and drive' no doubt represents the moral attitude of a large number of people, but the purpose of uttering these words is not to inform, but to persuade and convince those whose moral attitude is different. The real meaning of these words is much nearer the command 'Do not drink and drive' than to any statement of fact about drinking and driving.

This imperative element in moral judgements is to be found even when they can have no direct and immediate influence on conduct. Moral judgements which are passed on historical characters can have no direct effect upon their behaviour. 'It was wrong of Hitler to invade Poland' is useless as a command to Hitler, but it may still have the power to dissuade others from breaking promises and causing unnecessary suffering. Great literature provides us with many examples of characters and situations which can be a source of moral enlightenment to readers today. As Professor Ayer says: 'In saying that Brutus or Raskolnikov acted rightly, I am giving myself and others leave to imitate them should similar circumstances arise. I show myself to be favourably disposed in either case towards actions of that type. Similarly, in saying that they acted wrongly, I express a resolution not to imitate them, and endeavour also to discourage others.'

Emotivists deny the claim that ethical words merely describe either natural or non-natural properties in a thing or an action, or even the mental attitude of the person who uses them. Ethical words do have a descriptive meaning, but their primary function, their specifically ethical function, is to express the attitude of the speaker and to influence, in some way, the behaviour of the person to whom they are addressed. Thus, when we say 'It was wrong of you to punch your brother', we are not describing some property which we intuit in the action, but are expressing what we feel about it and hoping to persuade you not to do it again.

5. REASONS FOR MORAL JUDGEMENTS

There now arises the difficult problem of how far it is possible to justify moral judgements if they are merely expressions of attitudes. The great attraction of all descriptivist theories, that is those which hold that moral words are purely descriptive of qualities, whether these are subjective or objective, naturalistic or non-naturalistic, is that, if they were true, they would enable us to prove the truth of our moral conclusions. If 'good' and 'bad', 'right' and 'wrong' really do describe properties of things or actions, then statements in which these words are used can clearly be true or false; they are empirical statements of a particular kind. But if they are nothing more than empirical statements, then they cannot tell us what we ought to do because there is, as we have seen, a logical gap between what is the case and what ought to be.

If the Emotivist is right, and we cannot talk of moral judgements as being true or false, this does not mean that they are nothing but instinctive and unconsidered expressions of emotion, without any rational justification. We may not talk of them as being true or false, but we can often give very good reasons why they should be accepted or rejected.

Many people, when they read in the newspapers 'Atom bomb dropped on Hiroshima!—Thousand skilled', were moved to protest and say 'It was very wrong to drop the bomb'. If they had been asked to give reasons why they thought it wrong, they might have said that it was obviously wrong because thousands of people suffered. Such a reply would be equivalent to saying that it is wrong to inflict suffering; that is, it would be an ethical judgement and not an empirical statement. It is possible to set out the argument in the following form:

> It is wrong to cause needless suffering.
> The atom bomb on Hiroshima made thousands suffer needlessly.
> Therefore it was wrong to drop the bomb.

This is a valid deductive argument.

> Major premise: An ethical judgement.
> Minor premise: An empirical statement.
> Conclusion: An ethical judgement.

From the fact, if it is a fact, that the atom bomb caused needless suffering, we can deduce that it was wrong to drop the bomb, but only because we accept an ethical judgement as a major premise.

In making decisions about what is the right course of action in any particular circumstance, two things are necessary:

1. We have to ascertain very carefully all the relevant facts of the situation.
2. We need to have some general moral principle.

(a) Factual Evidence

It should be quite obvious that we cannot hope to do what is right in a situation unless we know what that situation is. This applies whether the decision is a non-moral or a moral one. If I field the ball at cricket, and the batsmen are stealing a short run, the end to which I should return the ball in order to run out one of them depends on where each batsman happens to be. If I do not know the facts of the situation, I cannot know to which end I ought to throw the ball.

This applies equally to moral judgements. A headmaster who is debating with himself whether a troublesome boy should be expelled must first of all assemble the factual evidence which is available. This will consist of the history of the pupil's school life, as far as it can be ascertained—all his truancies, acts of defiance, infringement of rules—but, in addition, the headmaster has to assess the likely consequences for the pupil, and for the rest of the school, of whatever action he proposes to take. If the pupil is not expelled, he will further upset the work of the school and exert a bad influence on other pupils; on the other hand, if he is expelled, his anti-social tendencies may be strengthened and he may embark on a life of crime. It is very difficult to predict what the results of either action will be, but it is necessary to make the best prediction possible before one can be in a position to make a decision. The decision must depend on knowledge of all the relevant facts, but, when all these facts have been ascertained, no decision as to which action is right can be deduced from them alone. Even if one knew for certain what the outcome of expulsion or non-expulsion would be, no moral conclusion about what ought to be done would automatically follow.

(b) Moral Principles

In order to get a moral conclusion, we must have a moral major premise. If the headmaster accepts the principle that we should do all we can to increase human happiness, then his argument could be set out as follows:

Major premise: We should try to produce the maximum of happiness.

Minor premise: The expulsion of the pupil will produce more happiness than his non-expulsion.

Conclusion: It is right to expel the pupil.

In order to decide the right thing to do in a particular case, we need to know the relevant facts and to have the ability to estimate the probable effects of the actions open to us, and also we must have accepted some general moral principle. It is only when we have a moral, as well as a factual, premise that we can deduce a moral conclusion.

(c) Conflict of Principles

In many moral decisions we find that there often arises a conflict of moral principle. We probably believe it is right to tell the truth, but there are surely occasions when we are justified in telling what we call 'white lies'. As well as believing in the moral principle of telling the truth, we may also believe that we are morally bound to do nothing to diminish the amount of happiness in the world; and these principles sometimes conflict. If a father, who has only a short time to live, asks you about his son, do you tell him the truth if the son has just been sent to prison? Is it right to inflict unnecessary pain on the father? Would life be made any happier if we always told our friends what we conceive to be the truth about them?

Telling the truth is a moral principle which holds good as long as there are no very good reasons for overriding it by another moral principle. We consider it right not to break a promise, but would it be right to refuse to save a person from drowning in order not to break a promise to go to the cinema?

In deciding between conflicting moral principles, we find that some are of far more general application than others. To tell the truth and to keep promises are both subsidiary to the moral principle that it is wrong to cause unnecessary pain. We can defend certain principles by appeal to these more general ones. For example:

Major premise: It is right to increase the happiness in the the world.

Minor premise: Keeping promises increases happiness.

Conclusion: It is right to keep promises.

Also, when we have to choose between, for example, telling the truth and keeping promises, we may appeal to a more general principle, and decide that the right action is the one that is likely to produce the greater happiness.

But there must be an end to this process of appealing from the more particular to the more general. There must be some moral principles which are fundamental and which cannot be deduced from others. If I maintain that it is wrong to cause unnecessary pain, it is difficult to see what more general moral principle there could be from which it could be derived. If someone does not see that it is wrong, he can hardly be persuaded to change his attitude by being shown what the consequences of his attitude would be.

(d) Agreement on Fundamental Principles

Although there is much disagreement both on the purely personal and on the wider social and international levels about the morality of actions, there are good reasons for thinking that these disagreements are about intermediate aims rather than about ultimate values.

There are children in certain primitive tribes who kill off their parents before old age robs them of their full physical and mental powers, in the belief that they will continue to enjoy these powers in the next life. If the belief is true, can we be sure that the killing is wrong? The children love their parents, and put them to death only because they believe that, by so doing, they will promote their greater happiness. There is no fundamental moral difference between their attitude and ours; the disagreement is about the empirical consequences of an action.

If it is true that there is widespread agreement about basic moral principles, then disagreement about which one of alternative actions is right is, in reality, disagreement about the facts of the situation. If two people, who agree that happiness is an ultimate good, disagree about the morality of two actions, their disagreement is about which is the more likely to achieve their common end.

In practice, we cannot always relate moral decisions to these ultimate values. For one thing, it is never possible to estimate all the consequences of an action and, for another, if we always attempted to do so, we should find that everyday decisions would become an intolerable burden. It is only occasionally that we feel it necessary to appeal to ultimate values before making a decision. We assume that it is wrong to tell a lie, even though we may hold that this principle can sometimes be overridden by the more basic concern for human happiness.

6. BELIEFS AND ATTITUDES

If we are looking for some way of proving ethical judgements, as we can prove analytic or synthetic statements, we are doomed to disappointment; but from this we do not need to conclude that we can never give any good reasons why we should accept one moral judgement rather than another. 'We commonly think,' wrote Professor Sidgwick, 'that wrong conduct is essentially irrational, and can be shown to be so by argument; and though we do not conceive that it is by reason alone that men are influenced to act rightly, we still hold that appeals to the reason are an essential part of all moral persuasion.' He believed that to behave morally is to behave rationally; although we may not be able to persuade someone to listen to reason, and hence behave morally, nevertheless, wrong conduct is irrational conduct.

Hume, believing that morality is an affair of the heart rather than the head, wrote: 'It is not contrary to reason to prefer the destruction of the whole world to the scratching of my finger. It is not contrary to reason for me to choose my total ruin to prevent the least uneasiness of an Indian, a person wholly unknown to me.' For Hume, to approve or disapprove of an act is purely a question of feeling and emotion. If I should happen to feel that it is better that the world should be destroyed than that my finger should be scratched, reason cannot show that I am wrong. It can never be demonstrated that I ought to forego the most selfish private whim for the sake of some public good.

How do we decide between these apparently contradictory answers? Do moral judgements have their basis in reason, as Professor Sidgwick holds, or in emotion, as Hume maintains? It would seem that, when moral disagreements are basically about matters of fact, reason has an important part to play in resolving them; but when there is disagreement about the fundamental conceptions of what is good and bad, it cannot be resolved by the accumulation of more facts.

Let us imagine two people disagreeing about the rightness of giving money to an organization which sends food parcels to the starving millions of India. One of them might argue that the mere sending of food will serve only to keep more people alive long enough to have bigger families, with the result that in a very short time there will be even more people starving. He could argue that to send food without some attempt to control the growth of population would be to increase the amount of suffering in the world. The other could argue that the plight of the starving millions is so desperate and tragic that we must do something, here and now, and deal with the future problems when they arise.

They both agree that suffering is an evil, and differ only about the best way of relieving it. By rational discussion it is possible to work out what steps are most likely to achieve the end they both desire. But if one of them says that he sees nothing wrong in suffering, it is not possible to reason him out of his attitude, if he really does hold it. We could show him pictures of starving children or, even better, let him witness at first hand the suffering which starvation brings, but this would be to shock him, not reason him out of his attitude. We could work on his emotions, but we could not show him that he is being illogical, because the question of logic does not arise.

Although we often say that it is true that suffering is a bad thing, it is not true in the way analytic or synthetic statements are true. There are ways of getting people to accept logical and empirical truths, but we cannot persuade someone to change his attitude if he cannot see that cruelty is wrong. To fail to see this is to fail to respond emotionally to an act; it is to show a lack of feeling rather than a lack of intelligence; it is a failure of the heart rather than the head. To this extent Hume was right when he said that 'reason is the slave of the passions', but, in so far as the majority of moral disagreements arise from differences of belief about the facts of the situation rather than from any difference of basic attitude, Professor Sidgwick was right when he said that these can be resolved in a rational manner.

The Russian and American political systems seem to be, in theory at least, poles apart; but it is not always clear whether their leaders differ primarily about ends or about means; that is, how far their disagreements are about fundamental moral principles and how far they are the result of different beliefs about the empirical nature of the world. The Russians' belief in historical determinism and the supremacy of economic factors will naturally determine the way they set about building their society, just as the Americans' belief in the virtues of free enterprise determines theirs. Their policies are bound to be influenced by their factual beliefs about human nature and about the kind of environment in which man can reach his fullest development. But though the means may vary in the two societies, is there any reason to believe that the ultimate ends may not be the same? And when we get down to basic moral principles, is it not likely that both the Russians and the Americans believe that what they are doing is for the ultimate happiness of their peoples?

When people disagree about what is the right action in a given situation, or about what state of affairs is good, they are not usually content to shrug their shoulders and do nothing about it. This reaction may be all right where questions of good and bad in matters of taste are concerned, but morality is too serious a business to be taken so lightly. It does not mean that we must not be tolerant of attitudes different from our own, but it does mean that we have the right to try to bring those who hold these attitudes round to our way of thinking and feeling.

In authoritarian states, the whole machinery of government is directed towards discouraging attitudes that are contrary to the official line: in western countries, there are strong, if less overt, pressures towards conformism. But as children grow up they are less prepared to accept that actions are right or wrong just because they are said to be so by some authority. When they begin to think for themselves, they ask for reasons, they want to know why they ought to do one thing rather than another. What sort of reasons are there which can be brought forward with some hope of changing someone's attitude?

Let us take as an example a schoolboy who is preparing for an examination, but who is neglecting his studies. The teacher says to him, 'You ought to work much harder, or you will fail your examination.' Now, as we have already seen, it does not logically follow, from the fact (if it is a fact) that he will fail the examination unless he works harder, that he ought to work harder. There is no logical contradiction in accepting the premise, and denying the conclusion. We cannot prove that he ought to work harder, but we can point to good reasons why he should.

This can best be done by drawing the boy's attention to further facts which will follow from his failing the examination. We can point out that the examination is a necessary qualification for the job he wants; we can mention the unhappiness his laziness will cause his parents, or the pleasure it will give his rivals. It is by an accumulation of facts such as these, by pointing to consequences of which he may have been unaware, that we can best hope to make him acknowledge that he ought to work harder.

Our deepest concern about differences of moral attitude is felt with problems which have important social consequences. One such problem is that of capital punishment, about which society is sharply divided. One section of society says that a person who commits a murder (unless he can plead diminished responsibility) ought to be hanged, whereas another says that he should not. Is there any possible way of resolving their disagreement?

The answer to such a question depends upon where the area of disagreement lies. Any intelligent attitude towards capital punishment must be based upon a knowledge of certain relevant psychological and social facts. If one person bases his support for the retention of the death penalty upon the belief that, without it, the number of murders will increase, and another person thinks it should be abolished, believing that there will not be an increase in the number of murders, then their disagreement is not an ethical one, but about matters of fact. What is needed is that both sides should look afresh and dispassionately at all the evidence, and then review their attitudes in the light of this knowledge. If this fails to produce agreement, it may be because the evidence which does exist is not conclusive, or it may be that the evidence is rejected in order to preserve a fundamentally ethical belief about capital punishment which is held, not because of the effects it is thought to have, but on other grounds. For example, someone who believes that all punishment is in essence retributive would not be influenced in his support of capital punishment by any figures about the number of murders.

The belief that most of our moral disagreements can be resolved by reasoning increases tolerance and tends to discourage excessive dogmatism. We must not, however, underestimate the difficulty of persuading people to change their beliefs, because they are often firmly held for emotional and psychological reasons rather than because they have any foundation in fact. Nevertheless, it is because beliefs can be rationally discussed, and because they often determine moral attitudes, that we can hope, sometimes, to resolve moral disagreements.

7. WHY BE MORAL?

We have so far discussed disagreements which arise between people who have different ideas about what things are good or bad, and what actions are right or wrong, but what do we reply to the person who asks 'Why should I be good if it doesn't suit me?'

In the modern world, people are less willing than they were to accept a moral code on the authority of the church or their elders; they are realizing more and more that, ultimately, they have to make their own moral decisions. Such a change in outlook inevitably brings its own problems. When morality ceases to be made up of imperatives issuing from an authoritative source, doubt and perplexity often appear and the hitherto accepted reasons for behaving morally lose their power to persuade. In a society where religion and morality have been closely associated, it is inevitable that a decline in religious beliefs should be accompanied by changes in moral attitudes. It is, therefore, not surprising that, in the rapidly changing moral climate that we have today, there are some who challenge the very need for a morality at all.

The Greeks, more than two thousand years ago, were faced with a similar problem. Fifth-century Athens, like twentieth-century Britain, was a place of great change and remarkable fertility in the sciences and the arts, and the wide-ranging rational enquiries of the Greeks left no portion of their life undisturbed. The gods of ancient mythology failed to withstand the assault of reason and were no longer believed in by the educated classes. Conventional morality was left, as it is in our own day, without its religious support and subjected to attack from all sides.

Prominent among those who attacked it were the Sophists (from the Greek word meaning wisdom), who were teachers and exerted a great influence in fifth-century Athens. We learn about their teachings from Thrasymachus, a Sophist who appears in Plato's *Republic*. To the question why we should be good, he replies that it would be foolish to do anything which does not promote our own self-interest. Thrasymachus holds that conventional morality exists merely to promote the interests of the ruling classes.

'Each ruling class,' says Thrasymachus, 'makes laws that are in its own interests, a democracy democratic laws, a tyranny tyrannical ones and so on; and in making these laws they define as "right" for their subjects what is in the interest of themselves, the rulers, and if anyone breaks their laws he is punished as a "wrongdoer". That is what I mean when I say that "right" is the same thing in all states; namely the interest of the established ruling class; and this ruling class is the strongest element in each state, and so if we argue correctly we see that "right" is always the same, the interest of the strongest party.'

The natural deduction for Thrasymachus is that the only sensible code of conduct is for each one to pursue a similar policy of self-interest. As Professor A. E. Taylor explains: 'If you get the chance to gratify your passions without moral scruples, and can be sure not to be found out and made to suffer, you would be a fool not to benefit by your opportunity.' To the question 'Why be good?' the Sophist replies that there is no reason why we should; our first concern must be our own happiness, and this is best assured by selfishness.

Plato agrees with the Sophists that each one of us seeks primarily his own happiness, but disagrees with them about the best way of achieving it. Plato does not question that self-interest is the most important motive in human conduct, but argues that the best way of achieving happiness is to follow the path of virtue. Plato answers the question 'Why be good?' with 'Because it pays' or 'Honesty is the best policy'.

To say that happiness can best be achieved by following the path of virtue is to make an empirical statement, which may be true or false. Plato believed it to be true but, if it were false, he would be forced to admit that there would be no reason why we should be moral. If we should be moral solely on the grounds that it is the surest way to happiness, then it follows that, if being moral does not lead to happiness, there can be no reason for being moral.

It would no doubt solve many of our moral perplexities if the world were constituted in such a way that unselfishness, truthfulness, kindness and other virtues were always rewarded by happiness, and if unhappiness were the inevitable consequence of selfishness, untruthfulness and cruelty. But do we really believe that this is the case, and that Plato's contention is justified? It is quite true that if we are kind and considerate to others they are more likely to be kind and considerate to us; if we keep our promises to others they will probably keep their promises to us. It makes us all happier when other people like and respect us, and this liking and respect can best be obtained if we are not exclusively concerned with our own selfish interests. It is probably because we realize this that most of us are less self-centred than we might otherwise be; we are all to some extent aware that altruism is often enlightened self-interest.

But is it true that immorality invariably leads to unhappiness, or that a moral life is always happier than an immoral one? Are we quite sure that crime never pays; that the man who smuggles a gold watch through the customs, or the business man who makes false income tax returns, leads an unhappy life as the result of his action? And do we find that the person whose life is a model of rectitude is always happy? It is hardly possible to maintain that the millions who willingly sacrificed their lives in the last war did so because they thought it was the best way of achieving their own individual happiness.

All the evidence would seem to show that, although there is some basis in fact for Plato's claim, it is not a complete answer to the question 'Why be moral?'. Henry Fielding was probably nearer the truth when he wrote: 'There are a set of religious, or rather moral writers, who teach that virtue is the certain road to happiness, and vice to misery, in this world. A very wholesome and comfortable doctrine, and to which we have but one objection, namely, that it is not true.' We cannot avoid the conclusion that morality is not based solely on self-interest, however enlightened.

Another answer to the question 'Why be moral?' is 'Because you will be rewarded or punished in the next world'. There is little doubt that for the past two thousand years this has been the only possible answer for most people. It is, in fact, a supplement to the one which Plato gave; although it may not be true that it pays to be moral in this world, it becomes true when we take into account the world to come. This still remains an appeal to self-interest, with the reward not immediate, but deferred. Those who accept the religious beliefs on which such a hope is founded need look no further for an answer to our question, but in an age when an increasing number of people do not accept the belief that there are rewards and punishments in an after-life, this answer is not acceptable.

If self-interest is not a sufficient reason why we should be moral, is there any other which is? There is certainly no logical reason which can be used to convince the moral sceptic. Society does what it can, largely by a system of punishments, to ensure that moral behaviour and self-interest coincide, but there remains a considerable field of action where they violently conflict. It may pay us to observe the thirty-mile speed limit because we shall be fined if we do not and are caught. We might be tempted to swindle British Rail if we were not afraid of being caught and sent to prison. In these cases, morality and self-interest coincide. But we are often guilty of dishonesty or selfishness, or show an indifference to the feelings of others, without being any the less happy as a result.

Morality is essentially a product of the relationship of individuals with one another, and is ultimately based on feelings which are not primarily self-centred. Understanding and sympathy for others may or may not promote our own happiness, but they form the basis of all morality. To a person who asks 'Why should I promote the happiness of others if I gain nothing by so doing?' there is no answer. When we get to basic moral attitudes, reason ceases to have a part to play; neither logic nor empirical evidence can compel us to accept basic moral judgements. If we do not feel that cruelty is wrong, then there is really nothing more that can be said; for all morality is based on feeling.

Moral education should be primarily directed not towards the inculcation of moral rules but towards increasing human sympathy and understanding, and concern for the welfare of our fellows, so that our own happiness will be seen to depend on the happiness of others. We need to acquire an imaginative insight into their joys and sorrows, and to realize that, in the words of a character in Albert Camus' *La Peste*, 'Il peut y avoir de la honte à être heureux tout seul.'

FOR DISCUSSION AND ESSAYS

1. Consider the following as examples of attempting to derive value judgements from factual premises:
   a. Arranged marriages are liable to be offensive to the pair so married.
   Whatever is liable to be offensive is bad.
   Arranged marriages are bad.
   b. Homosexuality is unnatural.
   What is unnatural is wrong.
   Homosexuality is wrong.
2. 'Science alone cannot prove that it is bad to enjoy the infliction of cruelty.' (Bertrand Russell)
3. 'I am as certain that cruelty is wrong as I am that grass is green or that two and two makes four.' (Paton)
4. When you say that an action is right all that you are entitled to assert is that *you* approve of it.
5. Without religion there can be no basis for morality.
6. 'If God does not exist, everything is permitted.' (Dostoevsky)
7. 'Cherchons donc à bien penser, voici le principe de la morale.' (Pascal)
8. 'La bonne volonté peut faire autant de dégâts que la méchanceté si elle n'est pas éclairée.' (Camus)
9. 'Unless schools succeed in producing citizens who recognize that their well-being is dependent on the stability of society, and that this in turn implies that there may be occasions when they have to conform to standards they consider are irrelevant, accept loyalties which they regard as out-dated and acquiesce to a faith which is beyond their comprehension, then society might well disintegrate.' (E. S. Conway, headmaster, *Times Educational Supplement*, 20 May 1966)
   Do you consider that society needs to be, or ought to be, defended in this way?
10. 'In the end, the only rules that are of final value are those we make for ourselves, putting into them our own conviction of

right and wrong.' (Rev. K. G. Greet, Chairman, British Council of Churches Report on 'Sex and Morality')

11. 'It is of the essence of morality that it must always be in principle possible to raise about anything which is in fact proposed or commanded the questions: "Yes, but ought we to do it?"; "Is it really right?"' (Professor A. Flew)

12. 'I believe in anything that is necessary to correct unjust conditions . . . so long as it is intelligently directed and designed to get results.' (Malcolm X)

13. 'The moral authority of a God (as of any other authority, such as a sacred scripture or a church) can only come from our own moral decisions.' (John Wilson)

14. 'The responsibility for our ethical decisions is entirely ours and cannot be shifted to anybody else; neither to God, nor to nature, nor to society, nor to history. Whatever authority we may accept, it is we who accept it.' (Karl Popper)

CHAPTER 5

MORAL THEORIES

Basic moral principles are largely matters of feeling or attitude; if our fundamental conceptions of good and right differ, we cannot demonstrate by reason that one conception is true and another false. Nevertheless, we can make clear, both to ourselves and to others, just what we consider these basic principles to be; in other words, we can state what criteria we use for the moral judgements we make. If we wish to have a rational and coherent attitude to moral problems, we must be able to give some sort of answer to such questions as 'Why do you think such an action right?' or 'Why do you consider so and so good?' We need to be able to make explicit the grounds we have for thinking some actions right or wrong, and some things good or bad.

In their discussions of these questions, philosophers have taken two quite different points of view. On the one hand, there are those who believe that we must first of all decide what things are good, and that only then shall we be in a position to estimate what actions are right. According to them, right actions are those which produce the greatest amount of good, that is we judge the rightness of an action by its consequences, and not by any inherent qualities in the action itself. This is called the teleological, or end-view of morality.

On the other hand, there are those who believe that an action is right or wrong irrespective of any consequences it may have. According to them, the moral worth of an action lies in the action itself, and we decide whether it is right or wrong by the presence of a special moral quality which can be detected by an intuitive power with which we are all endowed, or because it conforms with or breaks a moral rule. This is called the intuitionist or rule-view of morality, and theories of this kind are usually classed together under the general name of Intuitionism.

I. TELEOLOGICAL OR END-VIEW THEORIES

Any theory which judges the rightness of an action by its consequences must have criteria for judging these consequences. We cannot go on indefinitely judging things to be valuable as means; there must be some point at which we stop and say what things are valuable in themselves, and not for what they lead to. Some things are good merely as means—they are instrumental goods; whereas others are good in themselves—they are intrinsic goods.

(a) Instrumental and Intrinsic Good

If we were asked to make a list of some of the things in life which we consider good, we should not all include the same things. We might, for example, mention money, health, friends, work, kindness, skill at games and so on. But when we say that money is good, we almost certainly value it for what it enables us to do, and not for the possession of the money itself. Money is good because it can be used to increase human pleasure, which means that it is an instrumental and not an intrinsic good. Even the miser, who jealously hoards his wealth, does so because this is his own peculiar way of obtaining pleasure. It makes good sense to ask someone why he wants money, but it seems rather odd to ask the same question about pleasure. Pleasure, it would seem, is good not because it is a means to some further good but because it is good in itself. It is an intrinsic good.

In all discussions of morality, it is important to keep this distinction clear in our minds. Many of the things we strive for in this life, and which we consider good, are not in fact good in themselves but merely as means to some further end which is good. In many spheres of activity, the failure to realize this is responsible for much wasted effort and sometimes even unnecessary suffering. The businessman who begins life with the belief that the acquisition of wealth is the surest way to obtain pleasure may end up by forgetting that money is merely the means, and may discover, only too late, that he can no longer enjoy the pleasure which money was thought to bring. There are schools where discipline, instead of being used as a means to ensure good learning, has become something to be valued for its own sake: an instrumental good is mistakenly looked upon as an intrinsic good.

There is more agreement among philosophers about what things are good than about whether they are good instrumentally or intrinsically. Health, for example, is a good, because without it we cannot fully take part in many activities which normally enrich human life. To this extent, health is quite clearly an instrumental good, for its value lies in its power to bring pleasure and happiness. Even if we look upon health as something to be enjoyed for its own sake, and not for what it enables us to do, it is still of value only in so far as it is enjoyed. It is this enjoyment of good health which is the intrinsic good; health is but an instrument to this end.

Those who take a teleological view of morality (i.e. judge actions by their consequences) are inclined to consider that human consciousness of pleasure or happiness is the sole intrinsic good, and that all other goods are instrumental. Intuitionists, without denying that happiness is intrinsically good, usually claim that beauty, freedom, virtue and justice, for example, are good in themselves, quite apart from any consequences they may have.

Professor Sidgwick, believing that beauty is only an instrumental good, wrote: 'No one would consider it rational to aim at the production of beauty in external nature, apart from any possible contemplation of it by human beings.' Professor G. E. Moore, however, took the intuitionist view and, in a famous passage of his book *Principia Ethica*, sought to refute Professor Sidgwick. 'Let us imagine,' he wrote, 'one world exceedingly beautiful. Imagine it as beautiful as you can; put into it whatever on this earth you most admire—mountains, rivers, the sea; trees, and sunsets, stars and moon. Imagine these all combined in the most exquisite proportions, so that no one thing jars against another, but each contributes to increase the beauty of the whole. And then imagine the ugliest world you can possibly conceive. Imagine it simply one heap of filth, containing everything that is most disgusting to us, for whatever reason, and the whole, as far as may be, without one redeeming feature. ... The only thing we are not entitled to imagine is that any human being ever has or ever, by any possibility, *can*, live in either, can ever see and enjoy the beauty of the one or hate the foulness of the other. Well, even so, supposing them quite apart from any possible contemplation by human beings; still, is it irrational to hold that it is better that the beautiful world should exist, than the one which is ugly? Would it not be well, in any case, to do what we could to produce it rather than the other?' For Professor Moore, beauty is an intrinsic good which has value even if it is never contemplated by man. This view is held by many, but it raises the question whether the words 'beauty' and 'ugliness' can have any meaning except in relation to man's experience of them, or whether it makes sense to talk of a beautiful or of an ugly world without first taking for granted the existence of human beings with their feeling for values.

This same difficulty arises when we consider whether moral virtues are good intrinsically or merely instrumentally. Kindness, courage, truthfulness, loyalty are qualities which we admire, but is that because of the qualities in themselves or because of the desirable consequences which usually follow from them? Whatever we may think of Moore's argument that beauty is a good thing even if there is no one to appreciate it, moral qualities quite clearly can have no meaning except in a human context. We cannot have kindness, courage, truthfulness and loyalty unless there are people who are kind, courageous, truthful and loyal. It is also true that we encourage these moral virtues because they tend to increase the total of human happiness. People are much happier if they are kind to one another than if they are unkind; in fact we are inclined to judge whether an action is kind or not by its results in terms of happiness. A father who can never bring himself to correct his children when they do something wrong may so damage their moral development that we should be inclined to say that he is not really being kind to them: there is some truth in the saying that it is sometimes necessary to be cruel in order to be kind. If we believe this to be the case, then kindness would seem to be an instrumental rather than an intrinsic good; indeed we are only prepared to apply the word to those actions which promote human happiness.

Courage, on the other hand, is a quality we can admire quite apart from any consequences it may have. We may not understand what makes men row across the Atlantic in a small boat or climb the north face of the Eiger, but we cannot help admiring the courage they show in the face of physical danger. Our admiration has nothing to do with the consequences of these actions, although those who perform them no doubt derive considerable pleasure from their achievement. Even when courageous actions have evil results, we tend to think that the courage displayed is in itself good in spite of our regrets that it is not used to serve better ends. The courage which the German U-boat commanders showed during the last war was in the service of an evil purpose, and thus instrumentally bad, but was it not intrinsically good? Is it not possible to condemn their actions and at the same time admire their courage?

Loyalty, sincerity and truthfulness are all virtues which may serve evil ends; we can be loyal to bad leaders as well as good, we can be sincere and yet be wicked; we can cause much misery by an unswerving determination to be truthful. That is, these virtues can all be instrumentally bad, but does this exclude the possibility that they may at the same time be intrinsically good? Is there nothing to admire in the loyalty of a Nazi to his Fuehrer, in the sincerity of a Dr. Verwoerd, or in the truthfulness of Alceste in Moliere's *Le Misanthrope*? If one is prepared to admire these qualities on those occasions when they increase the sum of human misery, then one cannot believe that happiness is the only intrinsic good; loyalty, sincerity and truthfulness, although they may sometimes be instrumentally bad, must also possess an intrinsic quality of goodness.

Those who take an end-view of morality would agree with Moore that: 'The only possible reason that can justify any action is that by it the greatest amount of what is good absolutely should be realized', but they would not all agree about whether pleasure or happiness is the only intrinsic good. That pleasure is intrinsically good no one denies, but the reader must decide for himself whether beauty, truth, freedom, virtue are as well. I cannot do better than close this section with a further quotation from Moore's *Principia Ethica*. 'Accordingly, I do not think we need be much distressed by our admission that we cannot prove whether pleasure alone is good or not.'

(b) Hedonism

The doctrine that human consciousness of pleasure is the only intrinsic good is called Hedonism. To judge actions in terms of pleasure may hardly seem the basis on which to build a serious system of morality; indeed puritanism, which still runs through much moral thinking in Britain, goes so far as to equate pleasure with sin. This is, I believe, because pleasure is often thought of as, at best, ephemeral and, at worst, discreditable indulgence. It is, of course, true that the deliberate search for pleasure is sometimes an expression of a selfish attitude to life and an indifference to the welfare of others, but this is merely to say that pleasure, although intrinsically good, may sometimes be instrumentally bad. If a man spends most of his money on drink and deprives his family of the necessities of life, the pleasure which he derives from his drinking is intrinsically good, but instrumentally bad because of its results.

Hedonism is further rendered more acceptable as a moral doctrine by a paradox which lies at its very centre. Even if pleasure is the only intrinsic good, experience tells us that it is not always to be found if we seek it directly. It is often a by-product, a kind of bonus which is added to many different types of activity such as the search for knowledge, the quest for beauty or the performance of kind deeds.

The above paradox does not, however, completely banish the feeling that pleasure is a slightly unworthy aim of human endeavour: a moral life is more often thought of as a denial of pleasure than as its pursuit. This same feeling is not present when we talk of happiness, and those who condemn people because they are pleasure-loving find nothing to criticize in the pursuit of happiness. There is, of course, a difference between happiness and pleasure; it is quite possible to live a life crammed full with pleasures and not to be happy. Happiness has a more permanent basis than pleasure and is less dependent on external and transitory causes. Nevertheless, happiness is, according to the Oxford Dictionary, 'a state of pleasurable content of mind', and it is derived from permanent sources of pleasure such as health, knowledge, family and friends. If we truly understand what happiness and pleasure are, there can be no reason for approving of the one and disapproving of the other. It is only if we forget that love and friendship, the appreciation of beauty and intellectual pursuits give the kind of pleasure that leads to happiness that we shall find it surprising that for the Hedonist the words are interchangeable.

Attempts are sometimes made to distinguish between different kinds of pleasure by classifying some as superior and others as inferior. It is thought necessary to do this because, unless pleasures can be arranged in some kind of hierarchy, it is not easy to refute Bentham's statement 'quantity of pleasure being equal, push-pin is as good as poetry'. It is difficult not to believe that the pleasure that poetry gives is in some way better than that derived from push-pin, but is the pleasure better because there is more of it or is it of a different kind? Is Beethoven superior to bingo because of the quantity or because of the quality of the pleasure provided?

If we attempt to distinguish pleasures from one another by their quality, then we must introduce the idea of an intrinsic good other than pleasure. We may say that the pleasure we get from listening to a Beethoven symphony is nobler and more elevating than that derived from playing bingo, but if we do so we are abandoning the principle that pleasure is the only intrinsic good. If we say that one pleasure is better than another because it is more noble, then nobility is something which we value for itself. We cannot differentiate between pleasures from the point of view of quality without having some further principle of selection, and then this principle becomes an intrinsic good. If what we value for itself is pleasure and pleasure alone, then we cannot say that one pleasure is better than another; we can differentiate between them on the grounds of quantity but not of quality.

Philosophers who agree that right actions are those which produce the most pleasure differ about whose pleasure we are talking about. There are those who hold that we must do those actions which will provide us, as individuals, with the maximum of pleasure. There are others who say that we must consult not only our own interests but also those of society at large, and that we must do those actions which produce the greatest happiness of the greatest number. The first theory is called Egoistic Hedonism and the second Universal Hedonism, or Utilitarianism.

(c) Egoistic Hedonism

There are two different forms of Egoistic Hedonism: (i) Psychological Hedonism, (ii) Ethical Hedonism. Psychological Hedonism says that we *can* choose only that which is likely to give us most satisfaction (pleasure or happiness). Ethical Hedonism says that we *should be foolish* to choose anything but that which is likely to give us most satisfaction (pleasure or happiness).

(i) Psychological Hedonism

This is a psychological, not a moral theory. It is descriptive, not prescriptive; that is, it describes what motives we do in fact have for our choices, it does not prescribe what choices we ought to make. It says that people are all made in such a way that they cannot avoid seeking their own pleasure. It is quite clearly foolish to consider different moral theories about what people ought to do if it is a psychological fact that there are only certain things that they can do. It is useless to urge someone to do his duty when this conflicts with his pleasure if he cannot avoid doing the action which gives him most pleasure. We must first of all try to convince him that he will obtain greater satisfaction (pleasure or happiness) from following the path of duty than from any other course of action; for unless he can be persuaded of this, the laws of his own nature will compel him to find satisfaction by doing something else. Jeremy Bentham, the nineteenth-century philosopher, thought we should recognize the truth of Psychological Hedonism. 'It is pointless,' he wrote, 'to expect people to behave in any other way; to get them to do something, you first have to make them sure that they will gain something out of it—money, position, prestige, or just personal satisfaction or a warm glow inside—for themselves.'

I think we should all be prepared to admit that this theory about human motives contains a considerable element of truth. Freud and others have taught us to be suspicious of accepting our own and other people's motives at their face value. We have come to realize that we often think we have a certain motive for doing an action, whereas if we look at ourselves more carefully and objectively, we are forced to admit to a quite different motive. There is no doubt that many people who live lives of public service do so because they enjoy exercising power or like to be in the limelight. Can we be sure that when we contribute to charity it is not more for the feeling of self-satisfaction it gives us than because of the concern we feel for others? The psychological hedonist pushes these discoveries about our motives to what seems a logical conclusion, and says that every choice we make and every action we perform is motivated by our own self-interest. He maintains that it is impossible for us to behave in any other way. There is, he believes, nothing to be proud or ashamed of in this; it is just a fact about human nature. He claims that even when we do things which are normally thought of as being altruistic, we only do them because we like doing them; if we make a great sacrifice for someone else, it is only because making this sacrifice gives us more pleasure than any possible alternative action.

Such a theory has an obvious attraction, for by it the altruism of others, which may sometimes make us feel uneasy, can be explained away as being in no way morally superior to our own selfishness, of which we are so often painfully aware. If we must always seek our own pleasure, we need no longer feel guilty about our own motives when we suspect we are being selfish, nor do we need to accept the professed motives of others when they claim to be altruistic. It would also seem to lead to the rather unfortunate conclusion that if we cannot help seeking our own pleasure, we may just as well do so with an easy conscience, realizing that everybody else does the same.

If the psychological hedonist confined himself to saying that, for all of us, our own personal pleasure is the motive for our actions far more often than we like to admit, we should feel compelled to agree with him. But when he claims that pleasure is the only motive we can ever have, he is giving a false account of why we do things and is not correctly describing the way we respond to our environment.

If we are hungry, we take steps to appease our hunger. Eating a juicy steak will remove our craving for food and will probably also give us pleasure, but our motive for eating the steak is hunger, and not the desire for pleasure. This is not to deny that the gourmet may have forgotten what it is like to be hungry and be primarily motivated by the expectation of the pleasure a meal can give; but for most people, most of the time, it is hunger which is the primary motive, the pleasure following only on the satisfaction of that hunger.

A student preparing for a university entrance examination may at times find much of the work tiring and irksome, but, if he is a good student, he will derive immense satisfaction from meeting the intellectual challenge and from his increasing awareness of new fields of knowledge. It would, however, be false to say that his motive for taking the examination is the search for satisfaction. Satisfaction, or pleasure, may accompany his efforts, but it is not the motive for them. The psychological hedonist makes the error of assuming that because pleasure follows the satisfaction of our desires, what we always and only desire is pleasure.

However, he may still argue that, even if pleasure is not the only motive, we always do what we want to do. If we frequently eat because we are hungry and not directly for the pleasure it gives, yet it is still true to say that we should not eat unless we wanted to. There is one sense in which it is obviously untrue to say that we always do what we want to do; and we often use the word 'want' in such a way that we cannot prove that a person wanted to do an act from the simple fact that he did it. Many soldiers on the battlefield, if they were asked what they want to do, would reply without hesitation 'Go home', but they stay on and fight; and we know just what they mean when they say they are doing something they do not want to do.

But such an argument does not really imply anything more than that we are often faced with the choice between alternatives, neither of which we want to do. A soldier may not want to fight; he chooses to do so only because the consequences of refusal are even more undesirable. If he runs away, he may be shot for desertion or at the very least sentenced to a term of imprisonment. He may survive with honour if he continues to fight, but if he deserts, he faces the likelihood of punishment and dishonour. He may not want to fight, but he finds fighting preferable to the only other course of action open to him. To avoid doing something because of the unhappiness it will bring is to be guided by the hedonist principle just as much as to seek happiness directly; the avoidance of unhappiness is essentially the same process as the search for happiness. Therefore, paradoxical though it may appear, the psychological hedonist's claim that we always do what we want to do cannot be disproved by saying that we sometimes do what we do not want to do.

The argument that we always do what we want to do, or, when we have to choose between unpleasant alternatives, that action which we dislike least, is sometimes thought to imply that all behaviour is inevitably selfish. Thus, two people might discuss the actions of a third person as follows:

A. C is amazingly unselfish; he is always going out of his way to help others. Only yesterday he spent several hours cleaning up old Mrs. Jones's garden.
B. It is quite clear why C goes around helping people; he just happens to get his pleasure that way.
A. But surely he helps them because he likes them and wants to give them pleasure. It is better than thinking only of one-self.

B. The pleasure he gives others is not important; what matters to C is the pleasure he himself gets out of his actions.

A. You believe, then, that there is really no difference between people who are altruistic and those who do selfish actions; in both cases they are merely seeking their own pleasure.

B. Certainly!

But we all know perfectly well how to distinguish a selfish from an unselfish person; we know the difference between someone who thinks only of himself and someone who is alive to the needs and interests of others. Both persons may derive the same amount of pleasure from their actions, but we must not overlook the significance of the fact that they obtain their pleasure in different ways. One parent may seek his pleasure by spending so much money on drink that his children go hungry, whereas another may derive his pleasure from denying himself and doing his best for his family; to call them both selfish is to abolish an important distinction which must be drawn between them, and which we need words to describe. If a person who devotes his life to those who are in need is to be called selfish, then that kind of selfishness is to be admired; we are not entitled to adopt a cynical position and say that because people may get pleasure from helping others they are not to be admired.

Whatever the motives for our actions may be, they cannot help being our own motives; whether we desire our own happiness or the happiness of others, the desires are necessarily our own. But we must not conclude from this that all motives and desires are of equal worth and that altruism is merely a particular form of selfishness. To accept the truth of the tautology 'A person's motives for an action must be his own motives' does not debar us from distinguishing those motives which are self-directed, which we call selfish, from those which are directed towards others, which we call altruistic. To say that every action we do is the result of a desire we have does not tell us anything about the kind of desire it is, and from the fact that it is our own desire we cannot deduce that it is selfish.

The desire we often feel to promote the interests of others is not essentially different from our desire for fame or riches. If I want to relieve the suffering of a friend who is in pain, it is not my own happiness or satisfaction I am seeking but the relief of my friend's suffering. We are not always selfish, but do naturally feel love and sympathy for others; nevertheless, without the pleasure which we derive from the expression of our love and sympathy, should we ever do actions which can be called unselfish? What makes a person selfish is not the fact that he derives pleasure from the satisfaction of his desires, but the kinds of things which give him pleasure. If he derives his pleasure from the happiness of others, this is just what we mean by calling a person unselfish. We cannot do unselfish deeds without the desire to do them, and it is the satisfaction of our desires which gives us pleasure.

There may be occasions when we do things for others not out of love or sympathy but from selfish motives. We may show a person a kindness simply because we know that in the future he will be in a position to do for us something we very much desire. A business man who sends one of his customers a box of cigars at Christmas in the expectation of increased custom in the following year is acting selfishly, because he is primarily concerned with his own interests and not those of his customers.

Psychological Hedonism does not, as is sometimes thought, destroy all basis for morality, but it does suggest that if we wish people to behave morally they must be shown that they can, on the whole, obtain as much pleasure and happiness from unselfish as from selfish actions. It suggests that moral behaviour does not need to be based on lofty ideals of self-denial but on the psychological fact that we can all enjoy showing love and respect to our fellow human beings.

(ii) *Ethical Hedonism*

Ethical Hedonism does not say that we are *compelled* always to seek our own happiness, but that *we should be foolish* if we did not do so. It is a moral theory, concerned with matters of value, not a psychological one, concerned with matters of fact. An Ethical Hedonist believes that he should always choose to do that action which will give him personally the greatest possible satisfaction in terms of pleasure or happiness. Whenever he is faced with possible choices, all he needs to do in order to decide which choice is right is to weigh up carefully which one will produce for himself the greatest balance of pleasure over pain. Unlike the Psychological Hedonist, who says that we cannot help behaving in this way, the Ethical Hedonist says that this is the way we ought to behave. If we have to choose between actions A and B, the right choice is the one which, in the long run, will give us the more pleasure or happiness. We must not imagine that this is always the one which gives the greater immediate pleasure; it is a sign of maturity to recognize the wisdom of sacrificing a lesser pleasure in the present for a greater one in the future. A student forgoes many pleasures while he is preparing for an examination in the hope that he may later enjoy even greater ones.

The theory that we should always pursue such a policy of enlightened self-interest is one which most people would consider to be eminently reasonable. Bishop Butler, the eighteenth-century philosopher, certainly thought so, for he wrote: 'Our ideas of happiness and misery are of all our ideas the nearest and most important to us . . . though virtue or moral rectitude does indeed consist in affection to and pursuit of what is right and good as such; yet, when we sit down in a cool hour, we can neither justify to ourselves this or any other pursuit till we are convinced that it will be for our own happiness, or at least not contrary to it.' Professor Sidgwick also thought it important to draw attention to the wide acceptance of the principle that 'it is reasonable for a man to act in the manner most conducive to his own happiness'.

Egoistic Ethical Hedonism is not, however, a defence of complete selfishness. Experience tells us that very often the surest way of promoting our own interests is to promote the interests of others. We can none of us live isolated from other members of society; we rely upon them for our very existence. The way they behave towards us will depend on how we behave towards them, and if we wish our neighbours to be kind to us, we had better make an effort to be kind to them. Any behaviour which is purely selfish is far from being enlightened. To follow a policy of enlightened self-interest requires a degree of thought and intelligence which seems beyond the capacity of most people, but there can be little doubt that the world would be a much happier place if its inhabitants, instead of being motivated by passion, prejudice and false ideals, determined to act rationally in their own best interests.

Nevertheless, the fact that the universal adoption of Egoistic Ethical Hedonism might increase the amount of happiness in the world cannot be used to defend it as a moral doctrine. It is not possible to defend a doctrine which says that the only good we should pursue is our own happiness on the grounds that it is the best way of achieving happiness for others. The theory that we should seek to achieve the greatest happiness of the greatest number is Utilitarianism, not Egoistic Ethical Hedonism.

Egoistic Ethical Hedonism does not say that we must concern ourselves with the happiness of others, but it does point out that it is very difficult to be happy alone. Butler even thought that to pursue a policy of benevolence is the surest way of promoting our own happiness, and that there is never any conflict between doing good to others and pursuing our own self-interest. He wrote: '. . . benevolence and self-love . . . are so perfectly coincident that the greatest satisfactions to ourselves depend upon our having benevolence in a due degree.' By suggesting that benevolence and self-love, virtue and happiness never conflict, Butler is giving reasons why we should behave morally, but he is not saying that virtue and personal happiness are synonymous. He clearly believes that we ought to be benevolent, whereas the Egoistic Ethical Hedonist believes that we ought only to seek our own happiness.

In spite of Butler's claim, we all know from experience that occasions sometimes arise when there is a real conflict between what we consider we ought to do and the course which seems to be indicated by consulting our own self-interest. The person who takes a stand on some moral principle often does so without considering whether his action will bring him profit or pleasure. A bank robber who succeeds in evading capture may attain happiness by his action, but we still say he acted wrongly. We do not judge his action to be right just because it made him happy.

As we saw in the previous chapter, a theory which says that we are justified in seeking our own happiness even to the extent of using means which will bring great misery to others can hardly be called a moral theory. The moral point of view is essentially disinterested, not selfish. A Roman emperor whose pleasure it was to throw Christians to the lions cannot be said to have behaved morally, because there are no moral grounds on which he could have claimed that his own pleasure should count for more than the intense misery of his captives.

The failure to be disinterested, which is the essential feature of

Egoistic Ethical Hedonism, makes the theory useless when we try to settle conflicts of interest by it. Ethical theories, in addition to telling us how to behave, should provide us with a basis for morally assessing the behaviour of others. If A, after consulting his own self-interest, does an action which conflicts with the interests of B, we cannot solve the moral problem which arises on the basis of a theory which is egoistic. If A and B come to us for advice over some disagreement, do we recommend a solution which promotes our own happiness or the happiness of A or that of B? A moral solution will be one which is completely disinterested between the claims of A and B, but this Egoistic Ethical Hedonism cannot provide.

Most moralists would have no hesitation in saying that Ethical Hedonism, in its egoistic form, far from helping us to solve our moral problems does in fact make them more difficult of solution by giving the impression that, if only we look after our own selfish interests, the interests of others will look after themselves. The truth of the matter, these moralists would claim, is that often we can act morally only if we deny our own pleasures and are prepared to sacrifice our own interests. Some would even go so far as to say that morality and pleasure do not coincide but are incompatible, the moral life being the life of self-denial, even mortification of the flesh and the hair shirt in some extreme examples.

Such an attitude, however, is responsible for much unhappiness, and it is to be doubted whether it has done anything to make people behave better to one another. Although the Egoistic Ethical Hedonist seems to misunderstand one of the essential characteristics of morality, namely that certain things may be right and others wrong irrespective of their effect upon our own happiness, yet he does face the fact that for most of us what we think we ought to do and what we think will bring us most happiness in the long term are one and the same thing. By acknowledging this fact about man's moral attitudes, he is often able to channel his natural love and sympathy for others into moral ways of behaviour with more success than the moralist who sees duty as something completely divorced from desire or pleasure.

(d) Utilitarianism

Jeremy Bentham, who first formulated the moral theory known as Utilitarianism, thought it was possible to demonstrate scientifically which actions are right and which wrong; his ambition was to set morals 'upon the sure path of science'. He made two basic assumptions with which he thought everyone would be bound to agree.

1. We all act in such a way as to obtain for ourselves the greatest pleasure.

2. That action is right which produces a greater balance of pleasure over pain than any other possible action; not for the agent alone, but for the greatest number of people.

The resemblance of these assumptions to the principles of Egoistic Hedonism will be apparent. The first of them is the basic principle of Psychological Hedonism and is therefore an empirical and not a moral statement; the second is a moral statement of Ethical Hedonism, but it is not egoistic. For Utilitarians, happiness is the only intrinsic good, but it is the happiness of all people which matters, and not that of the agent alone.

The attractions of this theory for Bentham, who wished to establish a science of morals, are obvious. If we can measure the rightness of an action solely by the amount of happiness which results from it, it looks as if we have discovered how to distinguish between right and wrong by purely empirical means. In order to establish which of two actions is the right one, all we have to do is to assess as accurately as possible the consequences of the actions; the right one will be that which produces the greater balance of pleasure over pain.

If we accept Bentham's assumption, this is obviously the method to use; but, by giving 'right' a purely descriptive meaning, he has failed to show any reason why we should do one action rather than another. As we saw in the previous chapter, there is no logical connection between the empirical fact that an action will produce the greatest happiness and the moral conclusion that we ought to do it; we need, first of all, to commit ourselves to the moral principle that we ought to produce the greatest amount of happiness. Utilitarianism does not, therefore, justify Bentham's claim to have established a science of ethics.

Bentham was also faced with the difficulty of reconciling the assumption that we always act in our own self-interest with the further assumption that we ought to promote 'the greatest happiness of the greatest number'. This is the basic problem of all morality: how to make the step from self-interest to social duty.

If we are condemned always to seek our own happiness, how can we be induced to promote the happiness of others, which is what we ought to do?

Bentham thought that there is not usually any conflict between these two things because, on the whole, the world is constituted in such a way that we can best promote our own happiness by helping others. He thought that, for those occasions when we might be tempted to be selfish and neglect the interests of others, there should be systems of rewards and punishments which would make us realize that, even then, it would pay us to do what was right. This is in fact the basis of most societies. There are punishments prescribed by law which are intended to persuade people that they will be happier if they refrain, in certain specific cases, from being selfish and doing harm to other members of society.

Although Bentham failed in his attempt to turn morals into a science, he propounded a moral theory which, in different forms, has found wide acceptance and seems, on the whole, to agree most closely with the basic assumptions underlying common-sense morality. These are that an action is to be judged right or wrong by the end it serves, and that this end should be the greatest possible balance of pleasure over pain.

In practice, one obvious difficulty which the theory presents is that of working out this balance of pleasure and pain. If we cannot make a right moral choice without assessing the consequences of all the possible alternative actions, then we can never have adequate grounds for making a choice; for it is quite certain that we can never estimate the total consequences of any action. Nor can we judge later whether the action we chose was the right one, because we cannot know what the results would have been of the action we did not choose. Was it right to drop the atom bomb on Hiroshima, and is the rightness of that action to be determined by its consequences, as Utilitarians suggest? We know what some of the consequences of dropping the bomb were, but we do not know what the consequences would have been of not dropping the bomb. The bomb was dropped, and as a result thousands of people were killed and many are still dying slow, painful deaths from its effects. If it had not been dropped, the war might have lasted much longer and thousands of other people might have been killed who are alive today. It can never be conclusively demonstrated that one of these actions did cause or would have caused less suffering than the other, but if we accept Utilitarianism we have to act on such an estimate. Although we cannot possibly know what all the consequences of our actions will be, we have to act according to the best knowledge we can obtain. Subsequently we may discover whether we have acted rightly or not, but in many cases this is something we shall never know.

(e) Rule Utilitarianism

In more personal and minor moral decisions, where we might hope to estimate all the more significant consequences, we often find ourselves in a position where we do not have the time, or cannot be bothered, to make a careful assessment. For both these reasons, ordinary moral decisions are not usually reached as the result of a calculation of the possible consequences in each particular case. If a child is asked whether he broke a certain window, he may debate within himself the possible consequences of telling the truth and of lying. It is more likely, however, that he will tell the truth because he has been brought up to believe that it is right to tell the truth. That is, he will decide to follow a moral rule.

If we have a set of moral rules which tell us, among other things, that we must always keep our promises, be kind to others and tell the truth, we can the more easily take our moral decisions. As the result of moral education, these rules will have been so instilled into us that we shall obey them almost instinctively. But we must distinguish between why, on a particular occasion, we obey a moral rule and why we have the moral rules that we have. To ask why someone usually tells the truth is a question about motives, and is logically different from the question about the grounds he can have for thinking it right to tell the truth. Most of us usually tell the truth without assessing what the consequences will be, because we have been brought up to think that it is the right thing to do, but the moral rule itself may be based on the assumption that, on the whole, it is the best way of promoting the general happiness. We have, on the one hand, the empirical question of how we learn our moral rules and, on the other hand, the moral question of how we can justify them.

This form of Utilitarianism, called Rule Utilitarianism, saves us from having to estimate what the particular consequences will be every time we take a moral decision. Occasions may sometimes arise, however, when we are prepared to sacrifice a rule because it is fairly certain that it conflicts with the ultimate purpose of promoting happiness. In time of war we should feel justified, for example, in telling an enemy a lie if we thought that by so doing we could save the lives of our own men; the rule of telling the truth must be broken in these circumstances in order to preserve the more basic moral principle that we must ensure the greatest possible happiness. Although we may accept the rule that we must tell the truth, we must, if we are Utilitarians, believe that we are sometimes justified in breaking it.

We must not, however, forget that every time a moral rule is broken, the power which it has to guide our conduct is diminished. If we make a habit of telling lies whenever we think it is likely to increase happiness, we shall probably find that we are judging the rightness of an action by its most obvious and immediate effects and ignoring the long-term ones. If a pupil, whose chances of success at an examination are very slender, asks me whether he will pass or not, I can make him happy by telling him a lie, but his unhappiness will be all the greater when he finally receives his result. If he had been told the truth, he might have worked harder and even passed the examination. In addition, the faith of other pupils in my ability to assess their capabilities will be diminished and their general confidence may be shaken.

We accept moral rules because we believe that they have a general tendency to promote maximum happiness; we must not, therefore, break them unless there is overwhelming evidence that, by doing so, we shall produce more happiness than if we observe them.

The task of estimating the total consequences of an action is so great that the path of wisdom, even for the Utilitarian, is to deviate as little as possible from the moral rules. In practice, this is the way we all behave; we have been so conditioned by our upbringing to feel that certain things are right and others wrong that it is painful to act against these moral scruples; we are, in a sense, slaves to our principles. Nevertheless, when the Utilitarian is called upon to justify his moral decisions, he must appeal to the consequences and not to any absolute moral rule. The rules are a useful guide, but they do not contain their own justification.

2. INTUITIONIST OR RULE-VIEW THEORIES

For the Utilitarian the central concept of morality is the goodness of the consequences of an action, whereas for the Intuitionist it is the rightness of the action itself. The Utilitarian believes it is right to keep promises because doing so increases the amount of good in the world; the Intuitionist 'sees' that promise-keeping is right in itself. He believes that we have a special intuitive power by which we 'see' that a particular action is right, without any reference to its consequences. When the Intuitionist says that we 'see' that an action is right, he means to suggest that we have an inner moral faculty which tells us whether an action is right or wrong, just as our power of sight tells us whether a door is open or shut.

H. A. Prichard, one of the main proponents of this theory, says, 'The sense of the rightness of an action of a particular kind is absolutely underivative or immediate.' That is, when we decide that a particular action is right, it is not a conclusion we arrive at by a process of reasoning, but a truth of which we are directly aware. Right and wrong actions have characteristics which can be detected by an inner moral sense, just as physical objects have characteristics which can be detected by the physical senses.

Conscience

To this inner moral sense we give the name 'conscience'—a word we frequently use in moral discussions. We may say such things as 'I have a clear conscience' or 'My conscience is troubling me' or 'I can't do that: it is against my conscience'. We are generally more aware of the existence of a conscience in the negative than in the positive sense; that is, we are more fully aware of something within us which warns us against an action than of something which urges us to perform one. If we were to steal something, we should probably be more troubled by our conscience than if we failed to help someone in trouble. We may, on reflection, consider that the first promptings of conscience are not always a reliable moral guide and that it is worse to fail someone in trouble than to steal; nevertheless, in the majority of cases, it is in the performance of bad actions rather than in the non-performance of good actions that our conscience makes itself most keenly felt.

That we all have this intuitive feeling that certain actions are right and others wrong can hardly be disputed. It is difficult to see how anyone who says that he never experiences twinges of conscience can know the meaning of moral choice or understand what moral problems are. But having conceded that we all know what it is to have a clear or a troubled conscience, there still remains the problem of deciding just what it is and how it functions.

(i) Infallible Inner Voice

The Intuitionist claims that the conscience is a moral faculty which can always tell us whether an action is right or wrong, and that this is in fact the only way we have of deciding moral questions; if only we follow the dictates of our conscience, we are bound to do what is right. This view is widely held and forms the basis of the moral teaching of most religions. The inner voice, or conscience, is frequently identified with the voice of God, and it is a tenet of many religious faiths that God never allows a man's conscience to lead him astray.

The chief objection to the view that a man's conscience is infallible is the widely differing verdicts which it gives. There can hardly be a crime in the whole of man's long history which has not been committed in the name of conscience. The Inquisitors in Spain, or those who burned witches at the stake, were doing deeds which their 'inner voice' told them were right. We read with horror of the things they did but, in most cases at least, we cannot doubt their sincerity. When we look around today, we find that even those who believe in the infallibility of conscience do not agree about fundamental moral issues. Within the Christian Church there are pacifists whose conscience forbids them to take part in any war, but there are others who are prompted by their conscience to fight for what they believe to be right. We cannot reconcile these differences of belief by saying that what is right for one need not be right for the other, because the pacifist and the militarist not only believe differently but they also consider the behaviour of the other to be morally wrong. In such cases, how do we decide between the different verdicts of conscience?

To someone who says 'My conscience tells me that it is right to treat coloured people as inferior beings' we can suggest that he is not really listening to his conscience but to his prejudices and passions, and we can ask him to listen again. But if he listens again and comes up with the same answer, we cannot say that he is not really hearing the voice of conscience, for he is the only person who can decide what his conscience is telling him. Whatever our moral decisions, there are no independent criteria by which they can be judged, because the Intuitionist theory asserts that conscience is the sole source of moral knowledge. We have no means of telling whether we are correctly interpreting the voice of conscience except by consulting it as carefully as we can. It would never be possible to say, 'My conscience tells me that I ought to report my friend for stealing that money, but I wonder whether it is the right thing to do.' If we believe that it is only through our conscience that we can know the right thing to do, we can neither reject nor support the verdict it gives by appealing to another source of moral knowledge, for we have denied that such a source exists. Thus a person who, on grounds of conscience, says that suicide is always wrong is not justified in finding other reasons to support his verdict. If he claims that he has immediate awareness of the wrongness of suicide, he can only weaken his case if he tries to justify it on other grounds. He may, for example, say that suicide is also wrong because of its bad consequences, but then he is admitting that conscience is not the sole guide in moral affairs.

Any such attempt to combine Utilitarianism and Intuitionism into a single moral approach must show by what means we can reach a moral decision when the two different approaches do not give the same result. How, for example, do we reconcile the verdict of conscience that all wars are wrong and never justified with the utilitarian view that wars may sometimes be justified because of their consequences? These opposing views cannot in fact be reconciled, and we must either follow the voice of conscience or the principle of greatest happiness; we obviously cannot follow both these principles when they conflict. If we really believe that our conscience is the only source of knowledge about right or wrong, then we cannot also believe that Utilitarianism is of help in arriving at moral decisions.

(ii) *Voice of Society*

The theory that conscience is an infallible moral guide is difficult to reconcile with some of the ways it seems to function in practice. One of the most striking things about a person's conscience is the way it reflects the morality of the society in which he has been brought up. The variations of moral belief within a social group are much smaller than they are between one social group and another. There are members of certain societies whose conscience tells them it is right to kill off old men of the tribe, whereas there are other societies in which this is considered a wicked thing to do. This is difficult to explain except on the assumption that a person's conscience is, to some extent at least, the product of his environment. If this is true, it is not compatible with the theory that the conscience is a sixth sense which functions just like the other senses. The moral differences between societies separated by space and time have no parallel in the physical realm; we do not find members of different societies disagreeing about what they can see and hear as they do about what is right and wrong.

The view that conscience is the voice of society speaking within the individual accords with what we know of the way we acquire our moral standards. In our childhood the things we consider right and wrong are the things which are approved of or condemned by our parents and teachers. We learn that if we wish to retain the love of those around us, there are certain things we must do and others we must avoid. If the withdrawal of affection is the result of our doing certain actions, we shall gradually be conditioned to feeling uneasy whenever these actions are contemplated. This feeling of uneasiness may continue to be felt about doing things we no longer consider wrong.

Edmund Gosse, in *Father and Son*, gives several examples of the way a child is made to feel guilty about things which most of us would consider perfectly innocent. The following extract shows the spiritual anguish he felt at eating Christmas pudding. 'On Christmas Day of this year 1857 our villa saw a very unusual sight. My Father had given strictest charge that no difference whatever was to be made in our meals on that day; the dinner was to be neither more copious than usual nor less so. He was obeyed, but the servants, secretly rebellious, made a small plum-pudding for themselves. . . . Early in the afternoon, the maids—of whom we were now advanced to keeping two—kindly remarked that "the poor dear child ought to have a bit, anyhow," and wheedled me into the kitchen, where I ate a slice of plum-pudding. Shortly I began to feel that pain inside which in my frail state was inevitable, and my conscience smote me violently. At length I could bear my spiritual anguish no longer, and bursting into the study I called out: "Oh! Papa, Papa, I have eaten of flesh offered to idols!" It took some time, between my sobs, to explain what had happened. Then my Father sternly said: "Where is the accursed thing?" I explained that as much as was left of it was still on the kitchen table. He took me by the hand, and ran with me into the midst of the startled servants, seized what remained of the pudding, and with the plate in one hand and me still tight in the other, ran till we reached the dust-heap, when he flung the idolatrous confectionery on to the middle of the ashes, and then raked it deep down into the mass. The suddenness, the violence, the velocity of this extraordinary act made an impression on my memory which nothing will ever efface.'

An excessively narrow and puritanical upbringing may produce a conscience which will not be silenced even when a person no longer believes that what he is doing is wrong. Edmund Gosse's conscience continued to smite him every time he ate Christmas pudding even though he was convinced that it was not a wicked thing to do.

In order to understand the part which conscience plays in moral decisions, we need to distinguish between its origin, that is the psychological explanation of the way it is acquired, and its validity, that is the extent to which it can be relied upon to help us distinguish between right and wrong. Some people have a conscience which will never let them rest; as a result of an excessively strict upbringing they have a feeling of guilt about so many things that their lives are impoverished. The mere prospect of enjoying themselves may make them feel uneasy. There are others whose moral education has been so defective that stealing or lying does not occasion the slightest twinge of uneasiness.

3. SUBJECTIVE AND OBJECTIVE RIGHT

Members of a certain religious sect believe that it is morally wrong to receive blood transfusions and, as a result, many of them have died when, according to medical opinion, their lives could have been saved. Whenever they refuse such transfusions they are doing what they conscientiously believe to be right, yet most people would consider that they are doing wrong. Indeed, when the lives of children are at stake, the state feels justified in stepping in and overriding the wishes of the parents. And yet, if the parents acted in the way the state requires, they would be doing what they believe to be wrong. Can it ever be right for a person to do what he believes to be wrong? According to Father Coplestone, 'If our conscience tells us that we ought to perform a particular act, it is our moral duty to perform it.'

We have already suggested that when our conscience is the result of an over-strict upbringing it may sometimes tell us not to do things which, on reflection, we do not believe to be wrong. But if, in spite of this, we still believe that what our conscience tells us is the same as what we think is right, then it follows that it is right for us to do what our conscience dictates. In saying this, what is meant is that it is 'subjectively' right—it is right from the point of view of the person, or subject, who is doing the action. But if a person's conscience is not an infallible moral guide, it is possible for an action to be subjectively right and at the same time objectively wrong. We can say that someone who refuses blood transfusions on conscientious grounds is subjectively right, but objectively wrong.

When I am making my own moral decisions, I cannot distinguish between my own subjective idea of what is right and what is objectively right. Having to choose between two actions A and B, I cannot say, 'It is really right to do A, but I believe it is right to do B.' The action which I believe to be right must be for me the action which *is* right.

We sometimes admire a person for doing what he conceives to be right, even if we are convinced that he is misguided. This is especially so when the action is done against opposition or when it entails considerable inconvenience or suffering to the person himself. But when someone ruthlessly follows his own conception of rightness, even though it results in widespread pain to others, we call him a dangerous fanatic. History is full of such fanatics who have caused untold mischief by imposing on others their mistaken conception of right and wrong.

4. DUTY

The philosopher Kant believed that the only morally good actions are those which are done from a sense of duty. To save a friend from drowning because you feel affection for him is to do what is objectively right but, according to Kant, it is not a morally good or praiseworthy action. Only those actions which are prompted by a sense of duty, not by desire or inclination, have any moral worth. Such an austere conception of what is moral does not, I believe, correspond to the common-sense view. We frequently think better of those who do good deeds out of love for others than of those who coldly and deliberately do good because they conceive it to be their duty. In fact, the excessive conscientiousness of those who slavishly follow their duty is not always a characteristic to be admired. As Professor Nowell Smith writes: 'There is a story of an Oxford don who disliked Common Room life and whose presence caused himself and others acute distress. Yet he attended Common Room assiduously because he thought it his duty to do so. He would have done better to stay at home.'

It is often assumed in moral discussions that the terms 'right', 'duty' and 'what we ought to do' are equivalent. If I have a choice between doing A, which I believe to be right, and B, which I believe to be wrong, then we should agree that I ought to do A. But is it certain that occasions do not sometimes arise when we ought not to do our duty? If we believe that our duty and what we ought to do never conflict, how should we resolve the moral dilemmas which must have presented themselves to many Germans under Nazism? A soldier in the German army, with the fervent belief that it is his duty always to obey the orders of his superior officers, is ordered to shoot an innocent Jew. In spite of the poisonous teachings of the Nazis, he has not lost all moral sense and knows that to obey the order is to do something which is terribly wrong. He must choose between doing his duty and doing what he believes to be right; it is not obvious that he ought to do what he sees to be his duty, just because it is his duty.

A German Catholic bishop, in a letter about resistance to the Nazi war effort, took the view that the call of duty should override the verdict of conscience. He wrote: 'Are the greater heroes the Jehovah's witnesses and others who preferred to die in concentration camps rather than bear arms? All respect is due to the innocently erroneous conscience; it will have its reward from God. For the instruction of *men* I consider the greater heroes to be those exemplary young Catholic men, seminarists, priests and heads of families who fought and died in heroic fulfilment of duty . . . fulfilling the will of God at their posts just as the Christian soldiers in the armies of the heathen emperor had done.' But if we believe that it is the will of God that we should do our duty, even when it conflicts with our conscience, then we cannot also believe that conscience is the voice of God.

5. GENERAL RULES

Whenever we say such things as 'I followed my conscience', or 'My conscience told me it was wrong', we are thinking of particular moral decisions. We most commonly think of a conscience as something which responds to a concrete moral situation. Not everyone, however, is conscious of such a precise and immediate insight into a moral situation, and it seems necessary for those who claim that they are, to explain why people have such different moral insights into the same situation. If one person says, 'I can see directly that this action is right' and another says, 'I can see that it is wrong', there is no room for moral discussion and no way of deciding between them. For example, John Smith has promised his grandmother that he will call round after school and cut the lawn, but on the way there he meets his sister who tells him he must hurry home because his mother is ill. John runs home to his mother and puts all thoughts of grass-cutting out of his mind. If A says that he knows intuitively that John's action was right, and B says he knows it was wrong, and neither is prepared to give any reasons in support, then all they can do is to agree to differ. Indeed, if we do possess an inner moral faculty which pronounces infallibly on all moral questions, it is pointless to ask for further reasons.

On the whole, however, people are prepared to defend their moral judgements in particular cases by appealing to general rules. In the above example, A could defend his attitude by saying that it is right that children should love their parents and do what they can to make them happy; it was therefore right that John should rush home to see his mother. B likewise might appeal to a general rule, namely that one should always keep one's promise. John had promised to cut the grass for his grandmother, and that is what he ought to have done. A and B have now ceased to rely on a direct insight into a particular situation and have judged it as an example of a general principle.

Intuitionists who argue in this way say that, although we do not have immediate awareness of the rightness or wrongness of a specific action, we do have a moral sense which informs us of the truth of general moral principles or rules. Although our conscience cannot tell us directly whether it is wrong for someone to break his promise on a particular occasion, it does tell us that it is usually wrong to do so.

Now, if our conscience informs us of the truth of such principles as 'It is wrong to steal' and 'It is right to tell the truth', these principles must be always and universally true; there cannot be any exceptions. If we cannot apply them to all particular moral problems, we can never be sure whether the problem which faces us is an exception or not; and we study ethics to know what to do in practice.

Kant believed that it is always wrong to steal, lie, break promises and kill. The difficulty, however, with such a view is that when we come to apply these rules in practice, we sometimes find that in order to keep one rule we have to break another. If we believe that it is wrong to kill, we must also believe that we ought to do all we can to save life. But the principles of telling the truth and keeping promises sometimes conflict with the principle of saving life. We should not hesitate to break a promise to meet a friend in order to save someone from drowning; and although we believe that it is wrong to kill, we can all imagine circumstances in which we should be justified in taking another person's life. In practice, general rules are not always an infallible guide to action.

Because moral principles are of value only in so far as they are applicable to concrete moral situations, they must not be framed in such vague terms that they offer no clear guide to choice or action. The injunction to love one's neighbour is compatible with a wide range of human behaviour; people in the past have done all kinds of wicked things out of love. The white landowner in the southern states of North America no doubt loved his black slaves, but this did not prevent him from keeping them in a state of servitude.

The bishops of Norwich and Lincoln, in a letter to *The Times* about the Abortion Bill, wrote: 'Most Christians would regard

Christian compassion as a dogma of the church. Our problem is to interpret this dogma in terms of legislation so that the interests of compassion are in fact secured in the direction most likely to benefit individuals and society as a whole.' The bishops are saying that we cannot know intuitively that abortion is always wrong, but that we must be guided by a concern for the well-being of individuals and society as a whole. The rule that love and compassion should lead us to know what to do can be applied to a particular moral situation only by assessing what the consequences of our actions are likely to be. We cannot know how we should express our love in a particular case of abortion except by attempting to calculate the result in terms of the greatest good. If we claim that we know intuitively that abortion is always wrong, there is no difficulty in reaching a decision about a particular case, but if all that we can know is the general rule that we must show compassion, then it is difficult to see how we can decide the form this compassion should take, except by reference to the consequences.

The Utilitarian considers that moral principles should not be broken because, on the whole, breaking them decreases human happiness. He believes that all moral principles are subordinate to the one central principle that a right action is the one which produces the greatest amount of happiness; moral rules have no validity of their own, but are a means to an end.

The Intuitionist says that, even if we ignore the consequences of our actions, it is still right to keep promises and wrong to inflict unnecessary suffering. We do not need to assess the consequences of a cruel action to know that it is wrong. Certain acts seem to have an inherent rightness or wrongness which is not derived from any consequences they may have. If it were possible to have two worlds in which all the inhabitants were equally happy, but in one they constantly lied whereas in the other they always told the truth, we should consider the truthful world morally better than the other. This could not be so if happiness were the only criterion of intrinsic good.

It is still possible that such moral feelings are utilitarian in origin and justifiable only on utilitarian grounds, but that in the course of time we have become intuitively convinced of their truth. From the moral teaching we have absorbed and from our own personal experience, we have acquired an emotional attitude to untruthfulness and promise-breaking which may be more effective in regulating our conduct than any rational weighing-up of consequences. This would explain why the view of the Intuitionist is probably more in keeping with what most people believe about moral matters than that of the Utilitarian.

6. JUSTICE

The difference between the Utilitarian and the Intuitionist can be most clearly seen with regard to the principle of Justice.

The Utilitarian says that we judge actions by the amount of happiness produced, but he says nothing about the way it should be distributed. Is it better to give a lot of happiness to a few people or a little happiness to a lot of people? If a parent with two children can produce a greater total of happiness by treating his children differently, that is unfairly, than by treating them in the same way, what should he do? According to the Utilitarian he should be unfair. At the same time, however, it should be noted that the Utilitarian would argue that the surest way for a parent to achieve the maximum of happiness for his children is to treat them all alike. He believes that we should normally be fair in our dealings with people because the whole of man's experience, of which we have derived the benefit through our moral education, teaches us that it is in this way that we shall produce most happiness. That is, although justice is an important principle, it is only a means to an end.

The Intuitionist believes that justice is a principle in its own right and must be observed whatever the consequences. 'Fiat, iustitia, ruat caelum' (Justice must be done, even if the heavens fall) is his firm conviction and, being an Intuitionist, he also believes that we have an inner sense which enables us to distinguish justice from injustice—that we know instinctively whether an action is just or unjust.

However, when we look more closely at the concept of justice, we see that it is not a simple notion or idea, and that the word is not always used with precisely the same meaning. We sometimes think of it as the relationship between crime and punishment, as when we condemn a punishment as unjust because of its severity. Another part of the meaning of 'justice' is concerned with equality;

we think it unjust that people should be treated differently without some very good reason. And, finally, there is the notion of desert— it is unjust to punish someone for a crime he has not committed.

Let us look more closely at these three aspects of justice.

(a) Justice as Suitable Punishment

Justice is thought of primarily as something which is dispensed in courts of law. Certain punishments are laid down for certain offences, and it is considered unjust that a person should suffer a more severe or more lenient penalty than is legally prescribed. There is an established relationship between a wrong act and the punishment which it carries, and this is determined by the gravity of the offence. To park a car in a forbidden zone is thought to be less serious than to drive a car without due consideration for others, and is less severely punished. At times, we may be shocked by a severe sentence because we feel that it views the offence with a gravity it does not deserve. At other times, we may believe that a punishment, by being too lenient, does not adequately express our disapproval of the offence. In either case, we feel that justice has not been done and our moral sense is offended.

But we do not have to go back very far in history to discover that our present idea of what is just differs considerably from that of our ancestors. Lady Wootton illustrates this: 'History', she writes, 'shows that there is nothing unchallengeable or permanent in assessments of the relative gravity of different crimes. You can see this clearly if you will look at some of the maximum penalties for various offences which are still written into our law, although I suppose nowadays nobody would dream of putting them into effect. A sentence of life imprisonment, for example, may be imposed, not only for murder, manslaughter, or rape; but also for the crime of stealing a letter from a post office or for damaging or destroying textiles; and the same fate has been prescribed for anybody who dares to maintain by spoken words the invalidity of the line of succession to the Crown. . . . One must accept the fact that these provisions were written into the law by responsible people who were, presumably, in their right minds. And the grotesque impression which they make today is a vivid reminder of how the gravest crimes of today may be regarded as trivial tomorrow—and vice versa.'

138

The fact that our idea of what is just varies from age to age and from place to place seems to cast doubt on the claim of the Intuitionist that we know instinctively the just relationship between crime and punishment. We consider a punishment just when it accurately reflects the level of our disapproval, and unjust when it does not. In the nineteenth century, offences against property received long sentences of imprisonment because of the almost sacred attitude of the time to private material possessions; illtreatment of children was less severely punished. In both cases justice was thought to be done, but it was not an unchangeable moral principle but a reflection of the values of the age.

Today people are slowly becoming aware of the seriousness of drunken driving, and with this growing awareness goes the willingness to look upon increasingly severe penalties as just. The reverse process is also at work, whereby the severity of a punishment induces the population to realize the seriousness of a particular offence.

All the evidence would seem to suggest that justice, in the sense we have been considering, is not a fixed relationship between crime and punishment, but something which is constantly changing because it reflects the changing values of society.

(b) Justice as Equality

If two motorists, without any previous convictions, are caught driving at 50 m.p.h. through a built-up area, justice requires that they receive the same punishment; to treat them differently if their offences are the same would be unjust. This feeling that justice means equality of treatment is not confined to legal penalties but extends to all aspects of social life. It is based on the principle that all human beings are, as individuals, of equal worth. If a schoolmaster treats a pupil with special consideration because he knows his father, or if a policeman manhandles a suspect because he is coloured, they are both denying by their actions the principle of justice.

During the last century, however, when slavery was at its height, this feeling was far less widespread than it is today. Although there are many parts of the world where people are still treated differently according to their race, religion and colour, an increasing number of people believe that equality before the law is an essential part of justice. But if we look upon justice as a moral principle of which we are instinctively aware, and if equality is part of what justice means, then we have to ask ourselves if there is any reason for restricting it to equality before the law. If we believe in equality of treatment, why not also in equality of reward? If justice is a principle of universal application, is it just that some men should have to toil hard and long for small material reward, whereas others do very little, but enjoy great wealth and luxury?

The unskilled labourer and the highly trained doctor are both serving society in their own way. If justice is an absolute moral principle, should they not then receive the same payment for the work they do? The lawyer has mental gifts which have been denied the labourer, but must society add its own injustice to the injustice of nature? There is no justice, that is no equality, in the way physical and mental gifts are bestowed upon individuals; there are some who are physically weak and deformed or mentally retarded, whereas others are strong and healthy or endowed with great mental powers. Is it just that society should be organized in such a way that those who lack physical and mental gifts are further penalized by receiving a smaller share of the world's goods? Is it just that society should be based on the principle 'To him that hath shall be given'?

Justice might seem to require that society should try, as far as possible, to put right the injustices which result from nature. This would mean that the unskilled labourer would be paid more than the highly trained doctor to compensate him for the harsh treatment he received at the hands of nature. The doctor, conscious of the fact that he started with an initial advantage, would willingly agree to a smaller share of material goods.

If justice, or equality, were an absolute moral principle, it would be right to do everything possible to ensure that everyone shared equally in the good things of this life. Complete equality would be impossible in practice; nevertheless this would be the goal to aim at. It would not matter that a society organized on this basis was less efficient; it would not matter that there were fewer goods to be shared, provided they were shared equally. If equality is fundamental, then a society in which all its members are equally poor and equally miserable is to be preferred to one in which they are all richer and happier, but to differing degrees.

The fact that no society is yet organized in this way, and that few people would consider it desirable if it were, suggests that justice is not a moral principle which overrides all other considerations, but is subordinate to what we consider expedient at any particular time. Changes in customs and institutions which tend towards producing a more equal society gradually become incorporated into our conception of what is just. Today, equality before the law is the most significant part of the meaning of justice; but the time may come when we shall all look back on the present social inequalities as unjust, as some people do today. John Stuart Mill described this evolution: 'All persons are deemed to have a *right* to equality of treatment, except when some recognized social expediency requires the reverse. And hence all social inequalities which have ceased to be considered expedient, assume the character not of simple inexpediency, but of injustice, and appear so tyrannical that people are apt to wonder how they ever could have been tolerated; forgetful that they themselves perhaps tolerate other inequalities under an equally mistaken notion of expediency, the correction of which would make that which they approve seem quite as monstrous as what they have at least learnt to condemn. The entire history of social improvement has been a series of transitions, by which one custom or institution after another, from being a supposed primary necessity of social existence, has passed into the rank of a universally stigmatized injustice and tyranny. So it has been with the distinctions of slaves and freemen, nobles and serfs, patricians and plebeians; and so it will be, and in part already is, with the aristocracies of colour, race, and sex.'

Equality is desirable in so far as it leads to an increase in human happiness. A society in which there are extremes of poverty and wealth is less happy than it would be if there were more equality, but we should hesitate to favour one in which equality was complete if that meant a lowering of the general happiness. There are some who argue that a diminution of the total happiness would be the inevitable result of a completely egalitarian society; initiative, they say, would die and no one would make an extra effort, knowing full well that it would not be rewarded. There are others who claim that the members of such a society would be happier if only because many of the factors which cause unhappiness in a competitive society would disappear. Which point of view is correct can only be decided empirically; it is a factual matter based on two entirely different estimates of human nature.

There is no reason, however, to assume that the broad general movement towards greater equality will not continue, and that the attitudes which now stand in its way will not eventually be discarded. If this is so, equality, instead of conflicting with happiness, will contribute to a happier as well as a more just society. But it will be an equality which is accepted because of its consequences and not because of its inherent rightness. Once accepted, it will acquire the status of a moral principle, and we shall wonder how we could have tolerated a society which deined it.

(c) Justice as Desert

Many people would argue that, although equality is one element of justice, it is not the most important one. It is not just, they say, that all people should be treated equally, for the simple reason that some are more deserving than others. If one person is conscientious and works hard, does he not have a right to a larger share of this world's goods than someone who is lazy and makes as little effort as possible?

There is therefore a conflict between the principle of justice as treating people equally and justice as treating them as they deserve. John Stuart Mill draws attention to this conflict in his essay *Utilitarianism*: 'In a co-operative industrial association is it just or not that talent or skill should give a title to superior remuneration? On the negative side of the question it is argued that whoever does the best he can deserves equally well, and ought not in justice to be put in a position of inferiority for no fault of his own; that superior abilities have already advantages more than enough, in the admiration they excite, the personal influence they command, and the internal sources of satisfaction attending them, without adding to these a superior share of the world's goods; and that society is bound in justice rather to make compensation to the less favoured, for this unmerited inequality of advantages, than to aggravate it. On the contrary side it is contended that society receives more from the more efficient labourer; that his services being more useful, society owes him a larger return for them; that a greater share of the joint result is actually his work, and not to allow his claim to it is a kind of robbery; that if he is only to receive as much as others, he can only be justly required to produce as much, and to give a smaller amount of time and exertion, proportioned to his superior efficiency. Who shall decide between these appeals to conflicting principles of justice? Justice has in this case two sides to it, which it is impossible to bring into harmony.'

To aim at a society in which everyone is equally rewarded is to ignore completely that part of justice which seems to require that rewards should bear some relationship to ability and effort. We consider it only fair that a pupil who has worked hard and has been successful in his examinations should gain a place at university rather than one who has wasted his time and done badly in his examinations. We say that the one deserves further education because of what he has achieved and the effort he has made, whereas the other does not. But it sometimes happens that a very intelligent pupil carries off all the prizes without having to work very hard, for achievement is the result of both ability and effort. Although it is true that as a general rule the greater our efforts the more we shall achieve, some people achieve great things with little effort, while others need to struggle hard to achieve less.

Now, when we say that it is only just that some people should receive more than others because they deserve more, do we measure their desert by their ability or by their effort? In practice, most of the prizes in this world are given for achievement, irrespective of the effort involved, but can we say that the bright boy who is always top of his class without having to work very hard deserves the prizes more than other boys who make a much greater effort but are less well endowed with brains? Is it to a person's credit that he was born with abilities above the average, and what does it mean to say that he deserves the rewards which frequently go with such abilities? Does it make sense to say of someone of subnormal intelligence that he does not deserve great success in life? We admire outstanding qualities, both mental and physical, but is it just that people who are fortunate enough to possess these qualities should be further favoured by society? It is no credit to them that they have outstanding ability: they were just lucky in the parents they had or, as someone picturesquely put it, in the chromosomal lottery.

On the whole, we are inclined to feel that desert has more to

143

do with effort than with ability. Effort, we believe, is within the person's control and it is to his credit that he does the best he can; if he also possesses natural ability he should merely feel grateful for his luck. And yet to say that it is just to give extra reward for extra effort presupposes that we can determine what part of achievement is due to ability and what part to effort. The schoolmaster is frequently faced with the problem of deciding whether the pupil of modest achievement is intelligent but lazy, or industrious but not very bright. And how can we decide which of two people is making the greater effort? It is not difficult to measure the differences of achievement, but there are no reliable criteria by which we can judge effort. A pupil who fails to listen attentively in class because his vivid imagination carries him off into a private dream world may be making just as great an effort as another pupil who absorbs every word. The effort that the one has to make in order to follow half the lesson may be as great as that of the other who listens to everything.

The power to make an effort is itself an ability which depends, to some extent at least, on factors beyond one's control. Concentration, application and persistence, on which our efforts depend, are largely determined by our heredity and environment. If this is so, is it any more just to reward a person according to the effort he makes than according to the abilities with which he was born? The determinist, who believes that all our good actions are due entirely to good dispositions and habits, which themselves are partly inherited and partly due to the care of parents and teachers, would answer that there are no grounds for distinguishing in this respect between ability and effort. In fact, there seems to be no justice in making one person happier than another merely because circumstances beyond his own control have made him better. If this is true, maybe 'desert', in its commonly accepted meaning, is a concept which should be abandoned.

If we believe that it is just and fair to give greater rewards for greater ability or effort, that is if we believe that the essence of justice is desert, we cannot also believe that justice is equality. To say that there are grounds for giving more of the world's goods to some than to others is to deny that all people have an equal right to them. Before we can decide whether the Intuitionist is right in claiming justice as an absolute moral principle, we have to know what it means. If it sometimes means equality and sometimes desert, there must be a further moral principle by which we decide what is just on any particular occasion. The Utilitarian believes that we have such a moral principle: the greatest happiness of the greatest number. He believes that it is right to reward all people equally if, in the long run, it seems likely to increase the total of human happiness more than any possible alternative course of action. If, however, more happiness would result from rewarding achievement, no matter whether this were the result of ability or effort, then that would be the right thing to do.

The Utilitarian does not necessarily believe that it is just and fair to do this. He does not necessarily commit himself to the common notion of desert. He could be a determinist who thinks that the ordinary idea of desert is indefensible and yet be in favour of differing rewards on purely utilitarian grounds. As Professor Sidgwick wrote: 'The only tenable Determinist interpretation of Desert is, in my opinion, the Utilitarian: according to which, when a man is said to deserve reward for any services to society, the meaning is that it is expedient to reward him, in order that he and others may be induced to render similar services by the expectation of similar rewards.'

The Utilitarian does not deny that to act justly is a moral duty, as it is to act truthfully and with kindness, but he believes that when these moral principles conflict, as they often do, they are subordinate to the wider moral principle of increasing human happiness.

7. UTILITARIANISM OR INTUITIONISM?

When people begin to think seriously about moral problems and to wonder how they can justify their own moral beliefs, they find that they are faced with the choice of a utilitarian, or an intuitionist approach: the choice of defending their beliefs about right and wrong by referring to consequences or to rules. The fundamental difference between these two approaches is sometimes concealed by the fact that in practice they often function in the same way. The Utilitarian admits the difficulty of assessing all the relevant consequences of an action, and realizes that he can often be more certain that the observance of a moral rule will produce happiness than he can be about the consequences of any particular action. He can usually feel more sure about the general rule that telling the truth produces more happiness than telling lies than he can be about the consequences of telling a particular lie. This is not to say that he is never justified in telling a lie, only that he must feel very convinced that he can assess the relevant consequences of his lie before breaking the moral rule.

The fact that the Utilitarian and the Intuitionist both make use of moral rules in deciding specific cases must not, however, cause us to forget that they justify these rules in different ways. This difference is sometimes concealed by the Intuitionist who, although he claims that he has direct intuitive knowledge of right and wrong, may attempt to defend his position on occasions by reference to the consequences of an action.

The different approaches of the Utilitarian and the Intuitionist to moral problems can be illustrated by their attitude to capital punishment. What is interesting is that the division into supporters and opponents of capital punishment does not correspond to the two different approaches; we find supporters among Utilitarians as well as Intuitionists, and opponents among Intuitionists as well as Utilitarians.

Utilitarians do not all agree in their attitude to the hanging of murderers because they disagree about the results of doing so. Those who believe that by hanging murderers we reduce the number of murders support capital punishment, whereas those who believe that hanging merely increases the sum of human misery oppose it. Because they disagree only about the facts of the case, their disagreement is capable of being resolved. As evidence accumulates from our own experience, and from that of other countries where capital punishment has been abolished, we shall be able to settle conclusively which of these utilitarian positions is the right one. The Utilitarian cannot continue to maintain that hanging is justified on the grounds that it reduces the number of murders if in fact this is not the case. He may, of course, change his argument and become an Intuitionist, but as long as he remains a Utilitarian he must adjust his moral approach to the facts of the case. In the same way, if it can be shown that the number of murders increases significantly when capital punishment is abolished, then he must take this evidence into account.

The Intuitionist reaches his moral conclusion in the matter without any reference to the consequences. Some Intuitionists oppose capital punishment because they feel instinctively that it is always wrong to take a human life. This they firmly believe to be the case, and would not be shaken in their conviction even if it could be shown that there would be a large increase in the murder rate if hanging were abolished. Other Intuitionists support hanging, believing that the principle of justice is being infringed unless the murderer receives the only punishment which can atone for the wrong he has committed. They are intuitively convinced that unless a balance is maintained between crime and punishment, unless murderers get their true 'deserts', the whole basis of morality is undermined. As in the case of Intuitionists who oppose capital punishment, this attitude will be held irrespective of its social consequences; there is, therefore, no way of reconciling Intuitionists when they disagree, or of showing that one of them is right and the other wrong.

It is beyond the scope of this book to inquire into the different characteristics of temperament or upbringing which make people Intuitionists or Utilitarians, but these differences usually manifest themselves also in their general outlook on life. Rule morality, which by its very nature takes no account of changing social environment, is inevitably conservative. If, for example, pre-marital intercourse is thought to be wrong, not because of the danger of illegitimate babies but because it is wicked in itself, then its wickedness will not be abolished by the discovery of a perfectly safe contraceptive. The Intuitionist will, therefore, not see any reason why he should modify his moral position.

The Utilitarian understands that morality must change to take account of changing social patterns; he is, therefore, more radical in his approach to moral problems. Many of the moral arguments and disagreements of the present time arise from the clash between the conservative Intuitionist and the radical Utilitarian. The Intuitionist will resist change as long as he can, but when the Utilitarian can clearly demonstrate that a moral attitude is contrary to the public good and causes unnecessary suffering, resistance to change becomes very difficult. The intuitionist belief that certain forms of birth control are wrong is becoming more and more untenable in face of the rising world population with its attendant misery and suffering. So that even Intuitionists are prepared to recognize this and sometimes accept utilitarian arguments without realizing that by so doing they are weakening their own position.

Archbishop Heenan, considering the problem of birth control, once said: 'The fact is that although moral principles remain fixed and certain, we still await guidance from doctors, physiologists and other experts.' The guidance from doctors, physiologists and other experts must be factual evidence about the consequences of allowing or forbidding certain methods of contraception, but the Archbishop did not explain how this empirical knowledge can be relevant if moral principles remain fixed and certain. Rule morality and end reality can be combined only if the rule is sufficiently general for its application in a particular case to be decided on utilitarian grounds. What we cannot do is decide intuitively that contraception is wrong and then modify this decision on utilitarian grounds. The Archbishiop did not make clear whether his approach to this moral problem was intuitive or utilitarian.

Unlike the Intuitionist, the Utilitarian will be anxious to sweep away all those moral rules which do not obviously promote the general happiness. But very sweeping and wholesale changes in the field of morality, as in all other branches of social organization, are essentially irrational because of the impossibility of foreseeing all the effects such changes will have. Changes there must be, but they must be of such a kind that their consequences can be estimated with a reasonable degree of confidence. Professor Sidgwick made this point: 'I hold that the Utilitarian, in the existing state of our knowledge, cannot possibly construct a morality *de novo*, either for man as he is, or for man as he ought to be and will be. He must start, speaking broadly, with the existing social order, and the existing morality as part of that order: and in deciding the question whether any divergence from this code is to be recommended, must consider chiefly the immediate consequences of such divergence, upon a society in which such a code is conceived generally to subsist.'

Although the two moral approaches we have discussed may seem so different as to be incompatible, when we think about the way we justify our own moral beliefs we shall probably find that we do so from a position which is neither purely intuitionist nor purely utilitarian. In the first place we have to admit that, even if we believe that the moral worth of an action depends ultimately on its consequences, this belief itself rests upon an intuition. If we take an end-view of morality, we must hold that there are consequences which are good in themselves: that is, they cannot be justified by a further appeal to consequences. The Hedonist's belief that happiness is the only intrinsic good is basically intuitive.

The sharp distinction between these two approaches is further blurred by the fact that moral rules are considered to be of great practical importance even by those who take an end-view of morality.

The view that morality consists of following certain precise rules is the one which is most widely held by those who are less inclined to wonder about moral problems or to attempt to justify their moral attitudes. When, however, they are faced with a decision which is not clearly covered by a moral rule, or when two rules conflict, they usually appeal to utilitarian considerations both for obeying the rule and for breaking it. This would suggest that common-sense morality, although it gives the impression of being intuitive in so far as it is bound by rules, is basically and unconsciously utilitarian. Although people on the whole have an intuitive approach to morality, whenever they are faced with a difficult choice or have to enquire into the grounds for their moral beliefs, they show themselves to be Utilitarians. The growth of education and the increasing application of reason to moral problems cannot but hasten this process.

FOR DISCUSSION AND ESSAYS

1. 'Pleasure cannot be the only intrinsic good, because from our own experience we all know that a life devoted to the pursuit of pleasure soon produces boredom.'
2. The only good reason for a moral law is that its reign in a society substantially decreases misery in that society.

3. A community might say that the happiness of individuals is unimportant compared with the strength of the state. Would you agree?

4. No kind of act may be forbidden unless its discontinuance would lessen misery upon the whole.

5. I am inclined to pursue knowledge and truth, whatever the consequences in misery to the human race.

6. Misery is not the only evil and happiness not the only good. Vice is an evil and knowledge is a good.

7. One ought, other things being equal, always to do what makes for one's own pleasure.

8. Every man lives only for his own happiness.

9. Comment on the following popular song:–

> I want to be happy,
> But I can't be happy
> Till I make you happy too.

10. 'Utilitarianism is at once too simple in theory and too difficult in practice to satisfy either the philosopher or the plain man for very long.' (C. D. Broad)

11. 'In human affairs the means generally have to justify the end; ends are inferior carrots dangled before our noses to make us exercise those activities from which we gain most of our pleasures.' (C. D. Broad)

12. Judgements of morally right and wrong change with wider understanding of biological and social phenomena.

13. All moral attitudes are by their nature levelling and egalitarian.

14. 'The value of achievement is not compatible with that of equality. The value of achievement is inseparable from excellence, quality, and success in competition. The more highly equality comes to be regarded, the less room there is for achievement.' (Dr. R. Lynn.)

15. Equality is just a chimera, a nursery fable which nobody believes in and nobody wants.

16. 'There may always be good reasons why social justice should not be done, even where it can be shown that inequalities are unjust.' (Dr. W. G. Runciman)

17. 'We might feel inclined to give up the idea that justice has

anything to do with rewarding moral effort. It seems no more just to reward a person who is born conscientious than to reward a person who is born strong.' (John Wilson)

18. 'An industrial democracy means a nation in which men are equal in dignity and opportunity, but in which rewards go to effort, enterprise, brains, skill and qualifications.' (Quintin Hogg)

19. Discussing the future development of British universities, Professor Blackett said, 'We've got to be more non-egalitarian', because he believed that this is the only way of getting real excellence. Professor Robbins, on the other hand, is convinced that educational institutions should be as equal as possible. He does not understand how 'a government which is pledged to abolish artificial hierarchy and invidious distinction in the schools, should be actively engaged in preventing the elimination of artificial hierarchies in higher education.'

If a high degree of excellence can be achieved in only a small number of universities, do you think that certain ones should be singled out for special treatment or should they all be treated alike? In other words, do you think the principle of equality should override the utilitarian concept of efficiency?

20. 'In the last resort, what will count is a firm adherence to principle—based upon a moral judgement of what is the right course the government should take, *come what may*.' (*New Statesman*)

21. Would you defend the action of stealing from a rich miser in order to give the money to a poor man who is deserving?

22. Ought a man always to do what he thinks his duty even if he is wrong in thinking it his duty?

23. What is your attitude to censorship? If there were empirical evidence to show that violence in the cinema or on television encouraged violence in society, would you consider this relevant?

24. 'I know I have a conscience because it always tells me what is right.' Discuss.

25. Man should cure himself of allegiance to dead moralities.

26. Doing one's duty is only long-term selfishness.

27. 'A healthy appetite for righteousness, kept in due control by good manners, is an excellent thing; but to "hunger and thirst

after" it is often merely a symptom of spiritual diabetes.'
(C. D. Broad)

28. 'The right act is not the useful, or the dutiful act. It is the act
    that accords with a rule, and is therefore objectively ascertain-
    able.' (Sir Malcolm Knox)

CHAPTER 6

METAPHYSICS

There is little doubt that most non-philosophers consider philosophy to be primarily, if not exclusively, the study of those problems which we call metaphysical. The respect which is commonly shown to the philosopher is an acknowledgement of both the importance and the difficulty of the questions which he tries to answer, and the study of philosophy is thought to provide a kind of knowledge which cannot be obtained in any other way. It is widely believed that because philosophers are very learned and very wise they can answer questions which are too difficult for ordinary mortals.

We have all puzzled at some time or other about why there is a universe and how it came into existence; we have asked ourselves questions about *why* things happen as they do, and not just *how* they happen. The scientist tries to understand the world by studying particular things and events in the world; the metaphysician is not interested in this piecemeal approach, but seeks an explanation of the universe as a whole. The scientist is content to study the world of experience; the metaphysician believes that we cannot understand the world as it is without penetrating beneath what we perceive through our senses to something that lies beyond. For the metaphysician, the meaning of the world cannot be discovered by studying its separate parts; we can never learn *why* things are by following the scientist in his preoccupation with *how* things behave.

But, although metaphysics is primarily the study of a transcendental, super-sensible world which is not revealed to scientific enquiry, this is not the whole of it. There is a part of metaphysics which consists of certain fundamental principles or presuppositions, which cannot be derived empirically from observation or experiment but which help us to understand the everyday world of experience. That is, metaphysics, as well as providing, or claiming to provide, information about an order of reality beyond experience, also helps us to make sense of the reality we do experience.

I shall endeavour, as far as possible, to keep these two aspects of metaphysics separate, calling the transcendental aspect 'Knowledge of another world', and the non-transcendental aspect 'Understanding of the world of experience'.

I. KNOWLEDGE OF ANOTHER WORLD

(a) Deductive

From the time of the Greeks until the beginning of the modern scientific age, most philosophers believed that metaphysical statements could be shown to be true or false by a process of deduction, in the same way as we prove a theorem in geometry. The conclusion of a theorem in geometry is necessarily true, and it is this kind of necessity that the metaphysician claims for metaphysical statements. He believes that the statement 'God exists' is true in the same way as the statement 'The angles of an equilateral triangle are equal' is true.

But, as we have already seen, geometrical conclusions are necessarily true only because they do not tell us anything about what the world is like. They are derived from self-evident axioms, and their truth does not depend on the way things are, because they lack factual content. We cannot get more out of the conclusion of a deductive argument than we put into the premises; we can get a factual conclusion only if we have factual premises. But when we deduce factual conclusions from factual premises, we sacrifice the necessity which is found in conclusions from self-evident premises. For example, in the deductive argument:

> If you eat the sweets, you will be sick.
> You eat the sweets.
> Therefore you will be sick.

it is not necessarily true that you will be sick, because there is no necessity in the premises; it is by no means impossible that you may eat the sweets without getting sick. The conclusion cannot have a greater degree of truth than the premises from which it is deduced; and if the premises are empirical, that is, if they have factual content, they cannot be necessarily true.

If the metaphysician wants conclusions which are necessarily true, he must derive them from premises which are self-evident; but by doing so he sacrifices their relevance to the world as it is.

154

If, on the other hand, he wants his conclusions to be empirical, then he must derive them from empirical premises and thus sacrifice their necessity.

The logical impossibility of deriving empirical statements from self-evident premises has not, however, prevented metaphysicians from making the attempt. The best known of these is the onto-logical proof of the existence of God. The word 'ontological', from the Greek word 'ontos' meaning 'being', is used because what is being proved is the being, or existence, of God.

The premise of the argument states that no one can possibly doubt that, if there is a God, He must be a perfect being, for noth-ing less than perfection can correspond to our conception of what God must be like. But if God does not exist, He cannot be perfect, because he would be lacking in one feature—that of existing. It therefore follows that because God is perfect, He must also exist.

The self-evident premise from which the factual conclusion is supposed to be deduced is that, if there is a God, He must be perfect. But is this self-evident? There is nothing illogical or absurd in the belief that there is a God who is trying to do what He can for the world, but who is not powerful enough to overcome all the forces of evil. It may be precisely because He is not all-powerful, and therefore not perfect, that He needs man's help to accomplish his purpose. It follows that, if we reject the premise, we must also reject the conclusion.

Another objection is that, if we were to enumerate all the quali-ties which make anything perfect, we should not include among them the fact that it exists, since existence is not a quality. If, on a country walk, I came across an animal I had never seen before and tried to discover what it was by describing it to a naturalist friend, I might say; 'It was about two feet long with small, beady eyes and thick, grey fur.' If my friend asked for more information, I might say, 'It also had a long, bushy tail.' If, to a request for further details, I replied, 'O, yes, I forgot to mention that it exists', I should not be adding anything to what I had already said. In the same way, to say that God exists is not to say anything about God's attributes. It is quite impossible to reach any con-clusion about God's existence from the analysis of a definition.

Deductive reasoning from self-evident premises cannot lead to any conclusion about what does or does not exist. We cannot tell what the universe is like by a process of pure thought. This is true whether we are thinking of the real world we experience through our senses, or of some other reality which lies behind and beyond.

(b) Inductive

If metaphysical statements are not obtained by a process of deduction, maybe they are inductively true; if they cannot be derived from self-evident premises, maybe they depend upon observation and experiment.

Let us consider the statement 'The world was created by an all-loving God.' It is possible to argue that we have only to look around at the wonder and beauty of the world to realize that it must be true. There is certainly much in the world which can be used as evidence for such a claim: the beauty of nature, the marvels of the animal kingdom, the intelligence which allows us to ask such fundamental questions about the universe. All these seem to point to an all-loving Creator.

And yet there is also evidence which gives rise to doubts—the natural calamities of storm and earthquake, the way members of the animal kingdom prey upon one another, and man's inhumanity to man. These calamities may, of course, serve a purpose which we as ordinary mortals cannot understand, but this cannot be used as an argument here, because we are trying to show that it is reasonable to believe in an all-loving God by observing the characteristics of the world He created. If we set out to decide whether there is an all-loving Creator solely by seeing whether there is a preponderance of good or bad in the world, we cannot do so by dismissing all the bad things and saying that they serve a purpose which is hidden from us. If we do, we are no longer judging the issue on empirical grounds. Judged purely on these grounds, there seems to be room for doubt about the truth of the statement, 'The world was created by an all-loving God.'

But the metaphysician is not prepared to accept that this statement may not be true; he is not even prepared to accept that it may probably be true; he will settle for nothing less than that it is necessarily true. He demands, indeed, a degree of truth that empirical statements are logically debarred from possessing, and by so doing admits that 'The world was created by an all-loving God' cannot be shown to be true by the process of induction.

There is another reason for holding that the above statement is not empirical. When a scientist puts forward a hypothesis to explain observable facts, he is always prepared to say what particular facts would disprove his hypothesis. The physicist postulates the existence of electrons to help him understand the world, and is prepared to say that it is possible for certain things to happen which would show that there are no such things as electrons. Thus, he is prepared to say that if there are electrons, there will be certain precise consequences X, Y and Z. If X, Y and Z are not in fact the consequences, then electrons do not exist.

How would this apply to someone who believes that our knowledge of the world as it is constitutes sufficient evidence for the statement that the world was created by an all-loving God? If this is based on the evidence available, then it would be possible to imagine in what way the world would need to be different from what it actually is for the statement to be no longer true. If, for example, it is thought to be true in spite of all the suffering in the world, it is relevant to ask how much suffering there would have to be for it to be falsified. Would it remain true if half the world were laid waste and people were suffering from the aftermath of an atomic war? Would it still be true if all the world were devastated?

If the answer is that it would still be true whatever the world is like, then it would quite clearly not derive its truth from any empirical observations. If it is claimed that a statement is true whatever the condition of the world, the truth of this statement cannot be supported by any knowledge of what the world is like. This does not mean that the world was not created by an all-loving God, but only that, as a statement, it is not empirically true. It is impossible to establish the truth of an empirical statement by accepting all the evidence which supports it but none which will stand against it.

(c) Intuitive

This raises one of the most controversial issues of philosophy – are there any statements which we can know to be true other than analytic statements, whose truth is necessary, and empirical statements, whose truth is contingent? Is it possible to know that a statement is true even though there is no way of putting it to either

a logical or an empirical test? Once we have shown that the statements 'God exists' and 'The world was created by an all-loving
God' cannot be shown to be true, either by deduction or induction,
does it follow that there is no way of telling whether they are true
or not?

It is quite clear that we cannot rationally believe something to be
true about the world unless we can show in some way, that is by
producing some kind of evidence, why we hold it to be true. If we
believe that God exists, but do not believe that fairies exist, then
we must be prepared to give some reason why we believe the one
and not the other.

On the question of what we are justified in accepting as evidence,
philosophers are sharply divided. On the one hand, there are the
empiricists, who argue that all evidence is obtained by observation
through the senses; on the other hand, there are the metaphysicians, who believe that we have a power of intuition by which we
can find evidence of a world beyond the empirical. Metaphysicians
claim that we are not justified in assuming that the world of the
senses is the only world and that scientific or empirical statements
are the only ones which describe reality. May there not be another
reality behind and beyond the earthly reality we experience with
our senses; may there not be a metaphysical as well as a physical
universe?

Our knowledge of what exists is inevitably determined by our
physical make-up; we have five senses, and it is through them and
them alone that we experience what the world around us is like.
The world appears to us as it does only because we have the senses
that we have; if we possessed, or were to evolve in the future,
senses of a different kind, should we not have a different understanding of the nature of things? There are metaphysicians who
believe that we should not accept, *a priori*, the limitations to our
knowledge of reality which seems to be imposed by our physical
senses.

Plato believed that the ordinary, everyday world we discover
through our senses is only a world of appearances, and that behind
these appearances lies the world of reality, which is beyond the
reach of our natural senses. He took the view that all the knowledge
we obtain through our senses is imperfect and unreliable, and that
we must free our thought from all association with the body before

we can attain knowledge which is certain. 'If we are ever to know anything absolutely,' Plato wrote, 'we must be free from the body and behold the actual realities with the eye of the soul alone.' 'The eye of the soul', according to Plato, 'sees' the characteristics of the 'real' world behind 'appearances' in the way the natural eye sees the natural world: metaphysical statements are like empirical statements, but are about a different world and are observed by a special sixth sense, or intuitive power, which he called the 'eye of the soul'.

To illustrate the way the natural world is but a pale copy of the 'reality' which lies beyond, Plato presents the following dialogue:

'Imagine an underground chamber, like a cave with an entrance open to the daylight and running a long way underground. In this chamber are men who have been prisoners there since they were children, their legs and necks being so fastened that they can only look straight ahead of them and cannot turn their heads. Behind them and above them a fire is burning, and between the fire and the prisoners runs a road, in front of which a curtain-wall has been built, like the screen at puppet shows between the operators and their audience, above which they show their puppets.'

'I see.'

'Imagine further that there are men carrying all sorts of gear along behind the curtain-wall, including figures of men and animals made of wood and stone and other materials, and that some of these men, as is natural, are talking and some not.'

'An odd picture and an odd sort of prisoner.'

'They are drawn from life,' I replied. 'For, tell me, do you think our prisoners could see anything of themselves or their fellows except the shadows thrown by the fire on the wall of the cave opposite them?'

'How could they see anything else if they were prevented from moving their heads all their lives?'

'And would they see anything more of the objects carried along the road?'

'Of course not.'

'Then if they were able to talk to each other, would they not assume that the shadows they saw were real things?'

'Inevitably.'

'And if the wall of their prison opposite them reflected sound, don't you think that they would suppose, whenever one of the passers-by on the road spoke, that the voice belonged to the shadow passing before them?'

'They would be bound to think so.'

'And so they would believe that the shadows of the objects we mentioned were in all respects real.'

'Yes, inevitably.'

'Then think what would naturally happen to them if they were released from their bonds and cured of their delusions. Suppose one of them were let loose, and suddenly compelled to stand up and turn his head and look and walk towards the fire; all these actions would be painful and he would be too dazzled to see properly the objects of which he used to see the shadows. So if he was told that what he used to see was mere illusion and that he was now nearer reality and seeing more correctly, because he was turned towards objects that were more real, and if on top of that he were compelled to say what each of the passing objects was when it was pointed out to him, don't you think he would be at a loss, and think that what he used to see was more real than the objects now being pointed out to him?'

'Much more real.'

The cave dwellers did not realize that their physical situation prevented them from seeing the world as it really is; the shadows on the wall were, for them, reality, and the bright light of day dazzled and repelled them. Human beings in ordinary life, Plato thought, are placed in a similar situation by the limitations of their physical senses and, like the cave dwellers, they resist any attempts to dispel their illusion.

Plato's 'Simile of the Cave' is, of course, an illustration and not an argument; it gives us a vivid picture of what he means, but does not afford any evidence to show that what he says is true. When the metaphysician talks about an intuitive power which is aware of a reality beyond the empirical, he faces the problem, which confronts all those who make such intuitive claims, of making himself intelligible to anyone who does not possess such a power.

If a person is lacking any of the normal five senses, there is no difficulty in establishing this fact; there is also a procedure for resolving differences about the evidence we receive through our senses. The evidence from one sense can be checked by that from another. If two people look at an object, and one of them says it is made of wood and the other that it is made of metal, they can decide which of them is right through the sense of touch. But what can we say about this supposed intuitive power, or sixth sense, when we have no way of demonstrating its existence or of deciding between two people who intuit different metaphysical facts?

The type of metaphysics we have been discussing, which claims that we can have knowledge of a world beyond experience, has never recovered from the attacks of the philosopher, Kant, towards the end of the eighteenth century. He wrote: 'Undoubtedly there are many who, like myself, have been unable to find that this science (metaphysics) has progressed by so much as a fingerbreadth in spite of so many beautiful things which have long been published on this subject. Admittedly, we may find an attempt to sharpen a definition, or to supply a lame proof with new crutches, and thus to patch up the crazy quilt of metaphysics, or to give it a new pattern; but this is not what the world needs. We are sick of metaphysical assertions. We want to have definite criteria by which we may distinguish dialectical fancies . . . from truth.' It was by providing the criteria for judging whether statements are true, that Kant showed that metaphysical assertions do not add to the sum of human knowledge. The criteria which Kant provided are the ones we have used to show that our knowledge of what exists is confined to the field of possible human experience, and that metaphysical statements fail to pass this empirical test.

Nevertheless, Kant did not believe that the pursuit of metaphysics should be abandoned as a waste of time. 'However cold or contemptuously critical may be our attitude,' he wrote, 'we shall always return to metaphysics as to a beloved one with whom we have had a quarrel. For here we are concerned with essential ends.' He thought that the possibility of metaphysical knowledge was a '*natural* and inevitable *illusion* . . . but one inseparable from human reason'.

Perhaps the best way of looking at metaphysical assertions is not as statements, which can be true or false, but as hypotheses which perform a certain function in the business of living without ever attaining the status of knowledge. Father Coplestone seemed to take some such view when he wrote: 'Some philosophers would say that metaphysics consists in raising problems rather than in answering them definitely . . . I think that there is value in raising the metaphysical problems, quite apart from the question whether one can or cannot answer them definitely.'

Questions about another world or man's place in the ultimate scheme of things cannot be answered by the methods of science nor, perhaps, by any other method open to man. The answers we give will depend upon our feelings or our sense of values, and will always remain unproved and unprovable hypotheses. Our answers to any fundamental questions about the ultimate purpose of the universe, like our moral principles, derive from our conception of what is valuable in life. They will be hypotheses which will help us to make sense of the human condition rather than statements of metaphysical fact.

Such an interpretation of the essential nature of metaphysical assertions about a transcendental reality is in accord with the thinking of several present-day religious thinkers. For them, 'God is love' is not a factual statement about a supreme being, but another way of expressing the moral exhortation 'Love one another.' That is, assertions about an order of reality which transcends normal experience must be interpreted as recommending a moral attitude towards the reality we know.

2. UNDERSTANDING THE WORLD OF EXPERIENCE

Not all metaphysical statements, however, are hypotheses about some transcendental reality. In order to give meaning to the world we discover through our senses, we frequently make assumptions, or presuppositions, which go beyond what is warranted by the empirical evidence. Statements of fact can be checked by observation and experiment, but the systems we sometimes build on or around these facts may be proof against any test we may apply, or any evidence we may or could collect. Metaphysical statements and systems are not restricted to constructing another world beyond experience, but may serve as a framework to explain earthly existence.

(a) Metaphysics and Science

To understand the world, we need some way of organizing and arranging the multitude of impressions we receive through the senses. Unless we can see some pattern in things and events, all our individual observations must remain unconnnected and meaningless. But what reason have we for thinking that things and events do make sense, why should we assume that there is an order in nature?

Max Planck, the originator of the Quantum theory, wrote: 'We have no right to assume that any physical laws exist, or if they have existed up to now, that they will continue to exist in a similar manner in the future.' And yet surely this is something we do assume in our everyday lives as well as in all scientific studies. We believe that there is an order in nature which enables us to explain why things happened as they did in the past, and to predict what will happen in the future. Science presupposes that, in the words of Galileo, 'Nature acts through immutable laws which she never transgresses.' It is by discovering these laws that the scientist helps us both to understand and to control our environment.

In our everyday lives, we think we see a recurring pattern; we believe that there are regularities in nature which entitle us to assume that, because in the past certain causes produced certain effects, the same causes will produce the same effects in the future. It is because we are often successful in finding the causes of events that we think we are justified in saying that we understand them. But how do we know that there is an order in nature, and what right have we to assume that every event has a cause?

It is our right to the assumption that there are physical laws, and not their existence, that Max Planck was denying. He did not say that there is no order in nature, but that we have no grounds for thinking that there is; he did not mean that every event does not have a cause, but that we have no right to assume that it has. In other words, he was saying that the statement 'Every event has a cause' cannot be shown to be true or false.

We have seen that there are only two kinds of statement, analytic and empirical, whose truth can be clearly established. An analytic statement is true if it cannot be denied without contradiction, and an empirical statement is shown to be true by observation.

The statement 'Every event has a cause' is obviously not analytic, because it is possible to deny it without contradicting ourselves; there is nothing in the meaning of the word 'event' which compels us to deduce that it must have a cause. We may not believe that there ever are uncaused events, but they are not logically absurd as 'married bachelors' are.

If it is not analytic, perhaps it can be shown by observation to be empirically true. There is no difficulty in showing that particular events have particular causes, and as our knowledge of our environment increases we shall be more convinced that the general statement about cause is true, but the problem arises as to how many causal relations we have to observe before we are justified in making a statement about *all* events. As we have already found in the chapter on induction, we can never logically deduce a statement about all events from one about some events.

It is quite clear that we can never examine every event in the universe, but if we are to establish the truth of the causal principle, we must at some stage say that, having studied a very large number of events and not having found any which take place without a cause, we feel justified in assuming that there are no events which take place without a cause. If we had discovered that, in fact, certain events did take placed uncaused, we should have been obliged to abandon the causal principle; but could we ever discover that an event occurred without a cause? We might fail to discover anything to which we could give the name of cause, but the most this could prove would be that we had not discovered one. By further experiments and by refinements of techniques, we might subsequently discover a causal connection which had hitherto eluded us, but we could never dogmatically assert that there was *no* cause. Every time we succeeded in finding a causal connection we could claim that we had verified our statement, but it is of such a kind that it could never be falsified.

A general statement of this kind, which can be verified but which no empirical observation can ever falsify, cannot be known to be true. Does this mean that we must be prepared to admit that there may be events which are not caused? Quantum physicists, because they are unable to determine simultaneously the position and velocity of an electron, and hence to predict how it will behave, have suggested that causal laws do not apply to electrons and that their movements are random and uncertain. Whether this is so or whether it is because of a technical deficiency in our methods of observation, it runs counter to a conviction we hold, independently of experimental results.

The assumption that every event has a cause is a metaphysical one, it is a presupposition on which all our scientific knowledge is based. It is not a statement which can be true or false, but a metaphysical hypothesis, without which we could not begin to understand the world.

(b) Metaphysics and History

The task of the historian is generally thought to consist of describing what happened in the past. This inevitably involves selection of certain particular events out of the infinite number of events that took place, but this does not alter the fact that historical writing is basically empirical in that it is made up of statements which are constantly checked against the facts.

There is, however, a type of historical writing which is anti-empirical and which is not content just to describe events, but which seeks to make them intelligible in the light of some all-embracing pattern or purpose. The empirical historian makes use of the inductive process to discover various historical trends; he may even attempt to find a pattern, or historical laws which will enable him to predict future events; but these patterns or laws will arise out of his knowledge of what in fact happened. The metaphysical historian, on the other hand, starts with a grand design already in his head into which historical events have to be fitted. He makes the assumption that history must make sense, and the most obvious way in which this can be done is by explaining individual events as part of a wider purpose, or plan. Just as individuals have their own private purposes, so history as a whole is conceived as having some grand purpose, or goal.

When events are viewed in this light, they cease to be merely things that happened because of certain determining causes, and become inevitable and necessary as a part of a pre-ordained whole. An historical explanation becomes no longer a matter of explaining *how* things came to pass, but of showing *why* they *had* to come about as they did.

Such a teleological approach to history has a long and distinguished ancestry. Plato, referring to the naturalistic explanations of events in the writings of Anaxagoras, wrote: 'As I read on I discovered that the fellow made no use of Mind and assigned to it no causality for the order of the world.' Two thousand years later, at the beginning of the nineteenth century, the German philosopher Hegel also believed that behind the world as we see it there is a mind controlling events, and that if we want to understand anything we must see it as part of a rational process.

For Hegel, the basic reality of the world was mental, but for Marx, whose philosophy owed so much to Hegel's work, reality was fundamentally material. According to Marx, events must be explained not in terms of ideas or purposes but as the results of external, physical causes; the basic factors in historical change were economic and technical, and human choices and desires were of no significance in historical explanation.

The different patterns which Hegel and Marx professed to find in history were not discovered from the events themselves, but invented and then imposed upon history from without. They are not hypotheses which have been subjected to the empirical test of evidence, because they cannot be confirmed or rejected in this way. There is no way of deciding whether reality is fundamentally mind or matter, whether Hegel or Marx was correct. Both theories are metaphysical, because all empirical evidence is irrelevant to their truth; they are proof against anything that has happened or ever will happen.

An inevitable consequence of any attempt to explain events as serving an over-all purpose is that we cannot know how we ought to act unless we fully understand what this purpose is. Any actions which oppose the 'will of History' are doomed to failure, and the path of wisdom is to identify ourselves with the long-term goals of the historical process. When Mr. Kruschev said that the communists would bury the American capitalists, he was expressing his faith that history is on the side of the communists, and was using this metaphysical belief to give courage to his supporters and to instil fear into his opponents.

If all history is the working-out of a purpose, then nothing can ever thwart it; whatever is is best and necessarily so. The doctrine that the world we inhabit could not be better than it is was put forward by several philosophers in the eighteenth century. The evil which we think we see around us was thought to be either an illusion or of little importance. If only we viewed things in the right way, we should see that this is so. Alexander Pope expressed this in his *Essay on Man*.

'All nature is but art, unknown to thee;
All chance, direction, which thou canst not see;
All discord, harmony not understood;
All partial evil, universal good;
And, spite of pride, in erring reason's spite,
One truth is clear, WHATEVER IS, IS RIGHT.'

In these lines, Pope is not giving any statements of fact about the world as we know it; he makes no attempt to describe what is good or to show how he reached the conclusion that whatever is, is right. He is not, indeed, interested in 'what is', because he is not putting forward a hypothesis which can be shown to be true or false according to the evidence. What Pope is doing is to express a metaphysical belief, which does not rely on any facts and cannot be validated or disproved by anything we know or are likely to discover about what the world is really like. If the facts seem to suggest that the world is not perfect, then this must be because of our inability to see the facts in the right light; if the world seems to be full of discord, this is merely because we are unable to understand aright —discord is harmony not understood. To turn facts on their head in this way, to call 'all partial evil' 'universal good', is to decide beforehand that nothing empirical shall count against the belief.

One of the best-known expressions of this metaphysical belief is to be found in the writings of the philosopher Leibniz. Leibniz argued that 'Everything is for the best in the best of all possible worlds', and his belief has become more widely known because it was ridiculed by Voltaire in his story *Candide*. In this tale, Dr. Pangloss teaches Leibniz's optimism to his pupil Candide, but as the latter undergoes his adventures and sees all the pain and suffering in the world, he comes to the conclusion that to deny the existence of evil is to turn one's back on the realities of life. How, he thinks, can anyone who knows about the horrors of the Lisbon earthquake argue that everything is for the best?

Voltaire's satire is devastating; he describes in lurid detail some of the terrible sufferings which are a part of human existence, and shows that no one who looks at the facts can possibly claim that 'Everything is for the best in the best of all possible worlds.' But Leibniz's optimism cannot be demolished by the facts, because it does not pretend to rest on them but to be known independently of what the world is like. He believed that everything takes place in accordance with the will of a kind and loving God, and that, because we can never know all the facts, nothing that happens can ever justify our abandoning this belief.

For Leibniz, as for many others, metaphysical beliefs which help us make sense out of the everyday world cannot be separated from metaphysical beliefs about a transcendental, super-sensible world. They believe that we cannot understand the material world without postulating a spiritual one. Whether we think this to be so will depend on what sort of explanation we demand. The way we interpret our experience will depend on the kind of questions we think we can significantly ask. The scientist has given up asking *why* things happen and concentrates on the *how* of events; he has ceased to look for a purpose behind phenomena and contents himself with describing them. If we want to discover *the* meaning of life, and are not satisfied with the meaning which each individual is able to give to his own existence, if we want to view everything as the working-out of some grand purpose, then the scientific approach is not enough; we need to make metaphysical assumptions. But such assumptions will never be anything more than assumptions; they can never attain the status of knowledge.

Metaphysics, as a study, has been very much out of favour during the present century, especially among British and American philosophers, and it is difficult to see at present how it can ever again hold the dominant position which it held for so long. The scientific climate of the modern world is anti-metaphysical, and the successes which have followed from the empirical approach to our problems during the past three hundred years have inevitably contributed to the decline of metaphysics. Our attitude to metaphysical questions, just like our attitude to religious ones, is often a matter of temperament rather than rational persuasion. As Mr. G. J. Warnock writes: 'There is probably no other kind of writing, at least of a sort not primarily literary, so singularly liable to seem, at some times and to some people, so immensely important, and, at other times or to other people, so entirely useless. It would be impossible to deny that respect or distaste for metaphysics is, though no doubt it should be an intellectual matter, in fact very largely a matter of temperament; and disagreements of this variety are notoriously liable to be heated and vehement, liable also to be long drawn out, inconclusive, and rather unprofitable.'

CHAPTER 7

SOME CONCLUSIONS

I. DIFFERENCE BETWEEN KNOWLEDGE AND BELIEF

The most important development in philosophical thinking during the past two thousand years has been the clarification of the limits and scope of human knowledge. From the time of the Greek philosophers, for more than two thousand years, deduction was looked upon as the only way of obtaining truth about the universe. It was the syllogism, with its logical certainty, which provided the model for the acquisition of knowledge. From the seventeenth century on, the empirical methods of science were producing increasingly impressive results, but it was only slowly realized that deductive reasoning from self-evident premises provides no knowledge about the world.

Deductive reasoning, as expressed in logic and mathematics, still has an important role to play as a tool to manipulate the knowledge which observation provides. It is observation which supplies the premises, but logic is necessary to ensure that the conclusions drawn from them are valid. Precise methods of measurement, and the expression of laws in quantitative terms, require the assistance of mathematics. Thus, modern scientific knowledge is seen to require both deduction and induction, both reason and observation, but it is the change in the roles they play in this process which provides the key to understanding the difference between the scientific and the pre-scientific outlook on the world. With the realization that all real knowledge is scientific, the distinction between science and philosophy became much clearer. In those spheres where empirical methods could be applied, new sciences were born and knowledge was extended. The philosopher, whose province was once the whole of knowledge, now admits that this is the very field which he has been forced to abandon. All our factual knowledge is made up of true statements about the universe, and this is the realm of the scientist, not the philosopher.

We must not assume that because of this there is nothing left for the philosopher to do. Although we can say that all knowledge is obtained by a combination of deduction and induction, there are, beyond these limits, speculations of the human mind which are even more important in the power they have to influence human lives. How we should behave to one another and what we conceive man's destiny to be do not come within the province of the scientific, but they are none the less of passionate concern to man. They are, however, matters of belief rather than of empirical fact.

There is no precise dividing line between knowledge and belief, and what we only believe to be true today, we may know to be true tomorrow. What, then, are the main differences between knowledge and belief?

We have said that we test the truth of an empirical statement by observation and experiment; but how certain can we be that it is true? All our knowledge of the outside world depends ultimately on our senses, and principally on those of sight and touch. It is hardly possible to be more sure of something than of the existence of an object which we can immediately see and touch. If I see a book on the table, pick it up, examine it and put it back on the table, and then say, 'There is a book on this table', I have every reason for feeling sure that there is a book on the table. Nevertheless, it is possible that I am wrong, even in these circumstances. I may not have examined the object sufficiently carefully, it may have been a box which looked rather like a book. And yet, although the possibility of error is not totally excluded, it is difficult to imagine anything of which we could be more sure.

If I were to say, 'I saw a book on this table yesterday', I may also feel sure, but the grounds for feeling sure are not quite as solid as before because I have to rely on memory and not on immediate perception, and I may be remembering wrongly. It may not have been the day before, but two days before, and it may have been a different table. I may still feel sure that what I am saying is true, but the possibility of error is greater than if I am immediately perceiving the book on the table.

When we feel absolutely sure that something or other is the case, we say that we know it. If someone were to express doubt about whether the book really was on the table yesterday, I should probably reply, 'I know it was there', that is if I felt sure about it.

But if I realized that I had not looked very carefully, and could not be quite sure which day it was, then I might reply, 'I believe the book was on the table yesterday.'

One of the differences between saying 'I know' and 'I believe' is that in the former case I feel sure, whereas in the latter I do not; but this is not the only difference. It would be quite correct to say, 'I believe there is a book on the table', even if in fact there is nothing there, but I cannot say that I know, unless there really is a book on the table. If I believe that a statement is true, there is always the possibility that I may be wrong; if I know it, I cannot be wrong.

When I say that I know there is a book on the table, the grounds I have for feeling sure about it are that I can both see and touch the object in question. Many of the things we claim to know are not based in this way on immediate perception, but there must be evidence of some kind before we can say that we know them. If I pick up a soft, yellow pear and eat it and find it is sweet and juicy, I can report on my immediate experience by saying, 'This pear is sweet and juicy.' If, on several occasions, I eat soft, yellow pears and find them all sweet and juicy, I come to the conclusion that when pears are soft and yellow they are also sweet and juicy.

As we saw in the section on induction, I am making a generalization from my experience, that is I am going beyond what I immediately know, so that when I next come across a soft, yellow pear I say that I know it is also sweet and juicy. My encounters with pears of this kind in the past are my grounds for saying that I know what this particular pear will be like.

Much of our knowledge of the world is built up in this way, by generalizing from particular experiences. It is also quite obvious that some of these generalizations will be more satisfactory than others. If someone claimed to know what the weather would be like several months in advance, we should not be prepared to say he knew this, even though he said he was sure about it and it turned out to be true. Before we could say that he knew what the weather would be, we should want to know how he arrived at his forecast. If he based it on the abundance of berries on the trees, or on the state of his rheumatism, we should say that he was merely guessing about the weather and certainly could not lay any claim to knowledge.

Before we can claim to know something, three things are necessary: 1, We must feel sure about it. 2, What we know must be true. 3, We must have good grounds for thinking it to be true. It is quite clear that we do not feel equally sure about all the things we say we know and that the grounds on which our knowledge is based are stronger in some cases than in others. The second element, that of being true, never changes; if it is not true, it is not knowledge. But there is no clear and precise line which can be drawn between knowledge and belief. The main distinction is that we can believe, but not know, something which is not in fact the case. I can believe that the earth is flat, but I cannot know this, because the earth is in fact round. There is also the distinction that knowing something entails being sure about it, whereas believing contains an element of doubt. But just how sure we have to be before we are justified in saying we know cannot be precisely determined.

2. BELIEF AND EVIDENCE

The degree of certainty with which we can both know and believe something to be true depends on the quality and the quantity of the supporting evidence. We do not generally claim to know something unless we can produce evidence which most people are prepared to accept. Someone may say that he believes the bad weather we are having is caused by the nuclear tests, but he will hesitate to say he knows it, because he realizes he cannot produce any evidence for his statement which will be generally accepted.

People frequently hold beliefs for which they would find it impossible to produce any evidence, but because they are unable to do so it does not follow that the beliefs are unreasonable or that no reasons exist. It is not possible to ascertain whether a belief is a reasonable inference from the evidence until the evidence is expressed in the form of statements. If someone says 'I believe that the East Germans are very unhappy under communism', we shall want to know what reasons he has for holding this belief. If he then says 'I have no evidence, but I just feel that they must be unhappy', we shall not be likely to take much notice of what he says. On the other hand, statements such as 'Hundreds of East Germans escape to the West each week', 'There are long queues at all the food shops' and 'The suicide rate is rising every year' may be thought to be very good reasons for coming to the conclusion that the East Germans are unhappy.

Although it is unreasonable to believe something for which there is no evidence, most of us, at some time or other, do accept beliefs just because they are comforting and correspond with our wishes, and reject others because they conflict with what we like to think is the true picture of the world. The danger in such a procedure is obvious. Once we cease to look for evidence for the beliefs we hold, once we start to hold beliefs solely because they are comforting, then we have abandoned the only means we have for distinguishing between them. The fact that a belief is comforting may be considered a good enough reason for holding it, but it is no evidence at all for its being true. And once we give up the search for the evidence which will support the truth of a belief, we lose all means of distinguishing between one belief and another except by the comfort they provide. We must then openly adopt the position that we are not interested in whether beliefs are true or not, but only in whether they are comforting.

The study of the origins of our beliefs, why we believe what we believe, is a matter for the psychologist or sociologist; the logician is interested only in the relations between our beliefs and the evidence on which they are based. The psychologist and the sociologist explore the history of our beliefs and particularly what emotional or social factors give rise to them; the logician does not ask how we come to have our beliefs, but whether they are reasonable. We must try to avoid the error of thinking that the origin of a belief has any bearing on whether it is justified or not. It is sometimes argued that religious beliefs should be rejected on the grounds that they have evolved from primitive superstitious attitudes to the universe; but the truth or falsity of a religion is quite independent of how it originated.

The evidence which we possess for our different beliefs varies considerably. There are certain beliefs about which we have the right to feel sure because the evidence for them is so strong. There are others about which we may feel equally certain, but for which the evidence is very slight. If we wish to be reasonable about our beliefs, we must realize that we cannot hold them all with the same degree of certainty. Our belief that smoking cigarettes causes lung cancer is supported by considerable medical evidence, and if the evidence accumulates our belief will become all the stronger. It may even reach the stage when we shall be justified in saying that we know it to be true.

There are other beliefs which many of us hold for which the evidence is very slight, and sometimes even non-existent. I wonder how many people who believe that it is unlucky to walk under a ladder have any evidence to support their belief. There no doubt have been occasions when paint brushes or other articles have fallen from ladders and injured people passing underneath. It seems likely, however, that just as many have been injured by traffic when they have stepped into the road to avoid passing under the ladder. It seems extremely doubtful that there is any evidence to show that it is more dangerous to walk under a ladder than to avoid doing so. Those beliefs which lack any real supporting evidence we call superstitions, but where superstitions begin and reasonable beliefs end is not always easy to determine.

We are often justified in saying that we half believe something because there is not sufficient evidence to warrant anything more. This is a reasonable attitude to adopt and allows us to abandon the belief, or hold it more firmly, according to the additional evidence we receive. If at the beginning of a cricket season, I believe that England will win the ashes, I am unlikely to feel very certain of the outcome in a game as unpredictable as cricket, whatever my knowledge of the capabilities of the respective teams. In the event of an injury to England's best bowler, my belief will rest on even more slender foundations, and I may think it wise to give it up altogether.

This is the way we should hold our beliefs, always ready to modify them as the evidence changes. As people grow older, they are increasingly inclined to cling to beliefs for which there may once have been justification, but which are justified no longer. If we hold tentatively beliefs for which the evidence is not very strong, we shall find it much easier to abandon them when new evidence indicates that it is the reasonable thing to do. We can say that the reasonableness of a belief depends on the evidence we have for it, and the degree of certainty with which we hold it depends on its strength.

There is another criterion by which we can judge whether a belief is reasonable, and that is consistency. It is not reasonable to hold at the same time two beliefs which contradict each other. The human mind seems to be made in such a way that it is not difficult for us to keep certain of our beliefs in separate compartments of the brain, avoiding conflict between them by the simple device of ensuring that they are never placed side by side and compared. Some of us are more successful than others at this partitioning of the brain, but, whatever motives there may be for holding simultaneously beliefs which are contradictory, it is not a reasonable thing to do.

If we wish to be rational human beings, we must be prepared both to examine the evidence for our beliefs and to establish some degree of consistency among them. When two beliefs are seen to be contradictory, then the evidence must be re-examined and one of the beliefs must be abandoned. This is often very difficult to do and frequently gives rise to mental conflict.

It is often suggested that having beliefs is very desirable in itself and that it is less important what kind of beliefs a person has than that he has them. But there are no grounds for thinking that to believe, on the evidence available, that something is the case is in any way morally superior to believing it is not the case; they are both beliefs. This confusion has probably arisen from the two different meanings we give to the word 'believe'. In addition to believing *that* something is the case, we also say that we believe *in* something or somebody. Now, when we talk about 'believing in', we are referring to those things or persons we consider to have value or to be worthy of trust; we may believe in democracy or in someone's honesty. That we should believe *in* things, in the sense of having ideals, is very desirable, but this gives us no reason for thinking that to believe *that* anything is the case is other than morally neutral.

We also use the word 'belief' with the meaning of 'faith', in the religious sense. A person who has a religious faith is called a believer, and a person who has none an unbeliever. But this sense of 'believing in' or 'having faith in' a supreme being is quite different from believing that something is the case. In our present discussion, we are not concerned with belief in the sense of faith, but with believing that certain statements are true or false.

3. TOLERATION

Just as scientific theories are always tentatively held and abandoned once they are falsified by the facts, so our beliefs must always be open to modification if the evidence warrants it. Sometimes the very lack of grounds for a belief will make us cling to it all the more strongly if it supplies some emotional need. It is as if we know subconsciously that the belief is irrational, and try to compensate for the lack of evidence by a display of aggressive certainty. This is probably just as much to convince ourselves as other people.

The failure to realize that the strength of our beliefs depends upon the kind of evidence which supports them, and that this evidence can never be absolute and infallible, often leads to intolerance towards the beliefs of others. People persecute in defence of beliefs about which there can be no certainty, and precisely because there can be no certainty. No one is persecuted because he believes that the earth is flat, for the simple reason that most of us know the earth is round and are prepared to tolerate those who have such eccentric ideas. But beliefs about religion or politics or race, where there is no body of accepted truth, may produce intolerance. It is precisely because there can be no certainty in our beliefs that we must be prepared to tolerate the beliefs of others.

4. THINKING PHILOSOPHICALLY

'Philosophy is not a theory but an activity.'
(Wittgenstein)

To study philosophy is to engage in an argument, not to acquire any special kind of knowledge or wisdom; it is to question and to analyse, not to accept any particular doctrine or teaching. Wittgenstein, one of the founders of modern philosophy, wrote: 'Philosophy is a battle against the bewitchment of our intelligence by means of language.' The purpose of this book has been to provide some of the weapons which will help us to win this battle.

We must always be ready to ask 'What do you mean by . . .?' or 'It depends on what you mean by . . .', especially when abstract words like 'culture', 'democracy', 'civilization', 'poetry', 'equality' are used. We must guard against those who, by subtly redefining such words, hope to change our beliefs and attitudes. When someone talks about the 'real' meaning of 'culture', we must keep in mind that it does not exist, for a definition of 'culture' is a definition of a word, and not of a thing.

A study of philosophy also helps us to clarify what exactly we mean when we use such words as 'freedom', 'blame', 'responsibility', 'chance'. What is involved here is not a definition of these words, but an analysis of the concepts, or ideas, for which the words stand. For example, what can we mean by the concept of 'chance' in a world where every event has a cause?

But most of the 'bewitchment of language' derives from a failure to distinguish between the functions of different types of statement. Consider the following:

1. Democracy is rule by the people for the people.
2. Democracy was the form of government found in the Greek city states.
3. Democracy is the best form of government.
4. Democracy is the form of government approved by God.

Whether or not we believe all these to be true, we can see that they do not all perform the same function. The first statement is analytic because all it sets out to do is to give a definition of the word 'democracy'. It does not provide any factual information about any particular democracy, but tells us what characteristics a society must have in order to be called democratic. We may wish to give a different definition of the word, but before we can make any progress in a discussion of this subject it is essential to obtain agreement about what we take the word to mean. We shall never reach any useful conclusion if we persist in talking about different things.

The second statement is empirical, and can be verified or falsified by historical evidence. Discussions frequently go round in circles because the participants fail to take the rational course of checking the truth of their respective empirical claims. Facts should be verified, and not argued about.

The third example is a value judgement, and there is no way of demonstrating that it is true. We may produce evidence to show that people are happier under a democratic form of government than under any other, but this will not convince someone who does

178

not consider happiness to be the greatest good. If he were to maintain that totalitarian government promotes warlike qualities, and that a warlike society is preferable to a happy one, there would be no way of proving him wrong.

The fourth is a metaphysical assertion and, as we have already seen with assertions of this kind, it is far from clear how it could be shown to be true. It seems to be basically a value judgement expressed in metaphysical terms. One would certainly assume that the speaker thinks that democracy is a desirable form of government. By claiming that it is in accord with God's wishes, he hopes to remove it from the realm of personal attitude to that of metaphysical fact.

It is only if we make a distinction between the analytic, the empirical, value judgements and metaphysical assertions, that we can fully understand what is being said. Whenever anyone is attempting to persuade us to his way of thinking, we must distinguish between the statements he makes which can be verified or falsified and the other things he says which are merely the expression of attitude, and which cannot be true or false. Because facts and logic can win an argument more decisively than the expression of feelings and opinions, there is a great temptation to disguise the latter as the former. If I can persuade you to accept a value judgement as a necessary truth of logic or as an empirical statement, I am well on my way to getting you to agree with me.

When Jefferson wrote: 'We hold these truths to be self-evident: that all men are created equal . . .' he was trying to make people accept a value judgement by claiming that it is a necessary truth. 'All daughters have mothers' is a necessary, self-evident truth, but it gives us no factual information about either daughters or mothers. 'All men are created equal' is not a self-evident truth; we can deny it without contradicting ourselves, and we could not do this if it were. It would be absurd to say 'All daughters do not have mothers', but it would not be absurd to say 'All men are not created equal'.

If the statement is an empirical one, it is, on any ordinary interpretation of the word 'equal', false. Whether we are thinking of physical, mental or moral characteristics, it is undeniable that men are very differently endowed. On the other hand, all men are human beings and should be treated with equal respect and equally valued as individuals; they have equal rights to life, liberty and the pursuit of happiness. But this is a moral judgement, and not an analytic or empirical statement. It still remains a moral judgement even if we express it in metaphysical terms by saying 'All men are equal before God.'

The communists make use of this technique of disguising value judgements as analytic or empirical statements. They put forward the doctrine that there are necessary historical laws by which capitalism must inevitably be replaced by some form of socialism. But if this is a statement about the world in which we live, it cannot be necessarily true; if it is necessarily true, it can tell us nothing about the world. Only analytic statements are necessarily true, and these do not give any factual information; empirical statements are only probably true, and their truth can be tested by observation.

By claiming that historical laws are necessarily true, the communist hopes to avoid having to submit them to the test of empirical evidence. When we observe the way that the relationship between the capitalist and the proletariat has changed since the time of Marx, when we see that the proletariat, instead of becoming more and more oppressed, is enjoying an ever-increasing standard of living, we must conclude that the supposed laws of history are not empirically true either.

The communist, instead of trying to convince others of the attractions of the particular form of society which he himself admires, instead of admitting that he is making value judgements, hopes to bludgeon the opposition into accepting his own preferences as necessary historical laws.

We have already seen that value judgements cannot be logically deduced from empirical statements; we cannot deduce that something ought to be done from the fact that something or other is the case. From the fact that John is my brother, I cannot logically deduce the moral judgement that I ought to love him. But there are many words which have moral (or evaluative) as well as factual (or descriptive) meanings. Words like 'generous', 'unreliable', 'sociable', 'polite', 'cultured', describe certain personal characteristics, but they also carry the implication that these characteristics are good or bad, to be commended or deplored. As well as having a descriptive meaning, they have an evaluative one. If we say 'Jones is unreliable', we mean that he fails to keep appointments, does not do what is expected of him, and generally behaves in an unpre-dictable manner, but we also mean that we disapprove of this kind of behaviour.

Whenever we use a word which has both a descriptive and an evaluative meaning, it may seem that it enables us to deduce a value judgement from a statement of fact, and consequently demonstrate that the value judgement is true. To argue that conscientious objectors are unpatriotic and should therefore forfeit their rights as citizens is to attach the unfavourable emotive meaning of 'unpatriotic' to a particular descriptive meaning of the word. When the critic of the conscientious objector says that it is unpatriotic not to be prepared to defend one's country, he is making a value judgement rather than a descriptive statement. He is, in fact, using the word 'unpatriotic' in a very restricted sense to suit his special purpose. The dictionary definition of a 'patriot' is 'one who exerts himself to promote the well-being of his country', and the conscientious objector may believe he is doing just this when he refuses to fight in its defence. Whether or not he should be deprived of his rights as a citizen cannot be decided by calling him unpatriotic.

If we fail to realize that words are tools which serve different purposes, we may fall easy victims to one of the many false ideologies which are competing for our allegiance. This danger in-creases rather than diminishes as we grow more literate and can be avoided only if we maintain a critical, questioning attitude to what we hear and read. Such an attitude, however, is not incompatible with a sensitivity to the poetry and magic of words or an appreci-ation of the beauty of great literature. In the same way, a sceptical outlook which leads us to examine carefully the grounds for what we believe does not in any way preclude the possession of strongly held beliefs and ideals.

FOR DISCUSSION AND ESSAYS

1. 'There is no longer any need for God as a working hypothesis, whether in morals, politics or science.' (Dietrich Bonhoeffer)
2. We can never have explanations of the nature of things apart from our experience of them.

3. In Kant's phrase, we must not try to comprehend the incomprehensible.

4. The metaphysician is a man with an 'idée fixe' which he projects on the world in the form of an ambitious and distorted theory.

5. 'Causality is indeed one of the metaphysical requirements of physical theory.' (H. Margenau)

6. 'The world ceased to believe that Joshua caused the sun to stand still, because Copernican astronomy was useful in navigation; it abandoned Aristotle's physics, because Galileo's theory of falling bodies made it possible to calculate the trajectory of a cannon-ball; it rejected the story of the flood, because geology is useful in mining, and so on.' (Bertrand Russell)
   Does this account for the decline in metaphysics?

7. Any optimism, to be taken seriously, must make some attempt at an empirical analysis of nature in general, and of man in particular.

8. We need to enter into the thought of a metaphysician as we enter into that of a writer of imaginative literature.

9. Materialism is every bit as metaphysical as religion ever was.

10. 'When leaving the field of experience, our speculation can have no scientific status, since to every argument there must be an equally valid counter-argument.' (Karl Popper)

11. Speculation without the possibility of proof is superstition.

12. 'No scientific argument can ever have the slightest tendency either to prove or to disprove the existence of God.' Do empirical facts have any relevance to religious belief?

13. 'Statements are either certain and uninformative or informative and not certain. Metaphysical knowledge which claims to be both certain and informative is therefore in principle not possible.' (Sir Isaiah Berlin)

READING LIST

The following books are suggested for further reading.

(a) Not Difficult

Language and the Pursuit of Truth—John Wilson—(C.U.P.)
Thinking with Concepts—John Wilson—(C.U.P.)
Learning to Philosophise—E. E. Emmett—(Longmans)
The Use of Reason—E. E. Emmett—(Longmans)
Language, Truth and Logic—A. J. Ayer—(Gollancz)
The Problems of Philosophy—Bertrand Russell—(O.U.P.)
Elementary Formal Logic—C. L. Hamlin—(Methuen)
A Modern Elementary Logic—L. Susan Stebbing—(Methuen)
Ethics—G. E. Moore—(O.U.P.)
Human Freedom and Responsibility—Frederick Vivian—(Chatto)
Sex and Morality—British Council of Churches

(b) Rather More Difficult

The Fundamental Questions of Philosophy—A. C. Ewing—(Routledge)
Philosophy and the Physicists—L. Susan Stebbing—(Pelican)
Principia Ethica—G. E. Moore—(C.U.P.)
Ethics—P. H. Nowell-Smith—(Pelican)
Ethics and Language—C. L. Stevenson—(Yale University Press)
Logic and Sexual Morality—John Wilson—(Pelican)
Sexual Morality—R. Atkinson—(Hutchinson)
Ethics since 1900—Mary Warnock—(O.U.P.)
Equality—John Wilson—(Hutchinson)
Utilitarianism—J. S. Mill—(Many Editions)
On Liberty—J. S. Mill—(Many Editions)
Justice in Society—Morris Ginsberg—(Pelican)
Methods of Ethics—H. Sidgwick—(Macmillan)
Republic—Plato—(Penguin)